Discovering The

Discovering
The River Clyde

INNES MACLEOD
AND
MARGARET GILROY

JOHN DONALD PUBLISHERS LTD
EDINBURGH

ISBN 0 85976 333 1

British Library Cataloguing-in-Publication Data.

A catalogue record for this book is available from
the British Library.

Phototypeset by Newtext Composition Ltd, Glasgow.
Printed & bound in Great Britain by Scotprint Ltd, Musselburgh.

Contents

Introduction
and Acknowledgements

The main part of this book, Chapters 3 to 12, follows a topographical approach. We hope that it will be a useful, enjoyable and practical guide for discovering the River Clyde. The first two chapters provide an introduction to environment and history.

The Ordnance Survey Landranger maps 63, 64, 71, 72 and 78 at the 1:50,000 scale cover most of the places mentioned in the text. The Pathfinder maps on the 1:25,000 scale, for example sheets 446 and 431 for Lanark and Hamilton, are necessary for exploring the Clyde and Mouse canyons and gorges. Some six-figure map references have been given in the text for places that are difficult to find.

Walking in the gorges requires care and common sense. Details of your planned route should be left with friends for it is just as easy, given human frailty and vulnerability, to slide or bounce 150 feet downwards towards the Clyde as it is to go off Ben More, Assynt or Ben Nevis.

Many buildings and sites of interest are visible from the roadside or footpaths. Some are officially ancient monuments or reserves open to the public: others are on private land and permission for access and advice and guidance about local interests should be sought from the appropriate farm or estate before crossing fields and disturbing livestock. Dogs should be kept on leads and visitors in general should note that they are not really welcome on hill farms during the lambing season. The countryside is not, after all, some sort of 'heritage park' for 'hill walkers' and 'ramblers'. It is still essentially a workplace for far more people than may be immediately apparent.

We are very grateful for the helpful co-operation received and permission to reproduce photographs from:

Biggar Museum Trust pages 2, 4, 105; The Rev. G. Allan Collection, Biggar Museum Trust 7, 33, 40, 55, 80, 83, 87, 97, 99; The Hunterian Museum, University of Glasgow 17; The Royal Commission on Ancient Monuments, Scotland 37, 43.

59, 70, 89, 117, 118, 121, 139, 144, 172; Carluke and Lanark Gazette 49, 61, 68, 88; The University Library, University of Glasgow 58; Mr T. Burns 135; Mrs C. Cowan 141; Glasgow University Archives 170.

Other photographs, plates and prints are by the authors or from their collections.

CHAPTER 1

Mother Clyde

Many Scots at home and overseas think of the River Clyde with
an almost reverential regard, a maudlin affection, a sweet nostalgia
for lost reputations. She is not a mighty or destructive river. She
is on the whole rather small and gentle, kindly, motherly, reassur-
ing, a waterway on a very human scale, and full of surprises and
secrets. She runs for some 105 miles from her sources down to
the Broomielaw in the centre of Glasgow, and then another 28
miles to the open sea beyond Gourock. Somewhere between
Bishopton and the old Dumbuck ford near Dumbarton she
becomes the firth rather than the river. In this journey she goes
through an astonishing variety, a richness and diversity of scenery
and lifestyles from the vast bare stillnesses of Clydesmuir in the
south on to the green fields and wee villages of Clydesdale,
through terrifying ravines and chasms, between old orchards,
through the remains of poured out, disintegrating industrial
landscapes, between the clatter and culture of Glasgow, and into
the channel carefully cut by the Glaswegians to take her out to
Dumbarton and into the sea.

The last forty years have seen major economic changes with
the decline and virtual disappearance of traditional heavy industry
and mining in Glasgow and northern Lanarkshire and creeping,
but just as devastating, rural depopulation in the south. Farm
incomes are probably now generally in decline and prospects for
the future of agriculture are at least uncertain. Both Glasgow and
Clydesdale District Councils seem to have reached similar
conclusions about their economic profile for the 1990s. The
planned growth areas are to be in the service sector and in
tourism, the leisure and culture and heritage industry promoted
with some success in Glasgow as the European City of Culture in
1990 and with a comparable enterprise and imagination, albeit
with altogether more slender resources, by the Clyde Valley
Tourist Board, which is now supported by Clydesdale, Hamilton
and Motherwell Districts. One note of caution is that the population of 3 to 4 million people in the potential catchment area for

Sir George Reid (1841-1913), Clydes Burn from his series of sketches of *The River Clyde*, Edinburgh, 1886.

all-the-year-round trade is rather slight when seen in terms of the British tourist or heritage industry as a whole.

Clydesdale and the west of Scotland have in New Lanark, David Dale's and Robert Owen's utopian vision of the future, one world-scale tourist attraction. It will bring in visitors from England and France and Germany, from the United States and Japan, for many years to come. Glasgow may also remain a magnet for art lovers from Europe, America and Japan; but it is also quite possible that the interest in Charles Rennie Mackintosh and the Glasgow Boys, and even the French Impressionists, has already peaked. The assessments of art critics in calculating international market values and in laying down canons of excellence and good taste are, after all, notoriously fickle. It is perhaps expecting too much to suppose that these will remain constant into the twenty-first century. Glasgow does, however, have in the Burrell Collection another treasurehouse of mediaeval glass and tapestries, and new developments, for example a maritime museum centred on the Clyde which could attract enthusiasts from far afield, are always likely.

On a local, a Scottish and a United Kingdom scale, the Falls of Clyde and the Corehouse Nature Reserve at New Lanark and probably also the Forth and Clyde Canal have real potential for continued growth and are sufficiently special and spectacular to draw an ever-increasing number of visitors. Much more could be made of the 'Castles and Country Houses' along the Clyde, the Upper Ward mottes, Bothwell, Crookston, Craignethan, Newark and Dumbarton castles and Chatelherault; and the 'Christian Heritage Trail' label could be profitably attached to the early crosses and hogback stones at Govan in particular and at Hamilton, Dalserf and Luss, to important churches and pilgrimage centres including Glasgow Cathedral, Paisley Abbey and Carfin, and to the line of pre- and post-Reformation country churches in Clydesdale at, for example, Biggar, Carnwath, Coulter, Covington and Lamington. The museum complexes in Biggar, Glasgow, Hamilton and Leadhills are likely to experience further growth in response to the strong interest in local history reflected, for example, in the success of University of Glasgow Certificate courses in Scottish History and attendances at Extra-Mural liberal studies classes.

Strathclyde Region's 'River Valleys Strategy', which envisages an ever-expanding network of footpaths and footbridges and nature trails centred on the Clyde, the Kelvin, the Cart, the Calder and the Leven, dovetails well with local District plans to develop the Clyde Walkway from Glasgow Green to Lanark. Some sections, for example from Garrion Bridge to New Lanark, clearly represent at the moment a long-term aim rather than a facility currently available, but eventually a Clyde Walkway extending to Lanark and beyond through Thankerton and Wolfclyde and Lamington could link up with the Southern Upland Way at Daer Reservoir and Leadhills or at Beattock as it already does in the north with the Kelvin and the West Highland Way and the Forth and Clyde Canal. Perhaps it might also be possible to once again use some sections of the old drove roads, for example near Biggar or Crawfordjohn on the route south from Carnwath to Dumfries, or east by Dolphinton into Peebles-shire. There are already a number of riding schools and equestrian centres, for example at or near Carluke and Lanark, but there is still scope for providing opportunities for pony trekking, rough hill walking and orienteering on an organised and commercial basis. The Elvanfoot llamas are a most exciting and welcome recent initiative.

Sir George Reid, *Clyde at Abington* (1886).

More speculatively the future might see all sorts of new ideas and developments, for example a folk museum complex with reconstructions of working watermills, dovecots, farms, smithies, bakeries, tanneries (rather than more municipal museums); a wildlife park with Scottish and European animals, bison, bears, wolves, rare breeds of sheep and poultry and cattle, including some of the black-eyed, black-eared, black-muzzled Cadzow white cattle, and working horses, including of course the magnificent Clydesdales; a Roman fort or camp or a signal station fully excavated and then rebuilt beside a section of the Roman road parallel to the Clyde; a village of Iron Age or early mediaeval houses, taking the idea onwards from the recent school project at Coulter; an aquarium managed with the same flair and sympathetic understanding as the one at Skyreburn near Gatehouse-of-Fleet in the Stewartry of Kircudbright or a series of specially built ponds with breeding pairs of rare waterfowl as, for example, at Monrieth near Port William in Wigtownshire; or some open (hill) farms or orchards with glasshouses where city folk could learn about the realities of country life.

The River Clyde itself is already under pressure from the to some extent competing interests of water sports enthusiasts, the more traditional angling or fishing fraternity, ornithologists and botanists whose principal concern is the preservation of wetland and woodland habitats and other sites of special scientific interest, and landowners and farmers with an understandable concern over damage to property and livestock. Some congestion and problems over access seem inevitable, particularly on the stretches above Garrion Bridge.

The variety of uses made of the river is surprising. At Glasgow, between the Clyde Walkway Suspension Bridge and the Moat Hotel, the river is the scene of university boat races. Strathclyde Loch near Motherwell caters both for water sports enthusiasts and for pike, carp, eel, perch, roach and trout fishing. The upper Clyde is a mecca for serious white water canoeing, for example from the Strathclyde University base near Kirkfieldbank, and is also the venue of more fundamentally recreational fun runs.

The upper Clyde, for example the stretches near Kirkfieldbank, from Hyndford Bridge to Wolfclyde, from Thankerton to Roberton, and at Abington, is very much the preserve of trout-orientated angling associations allocating permits at a very moderate cost of some £10 to £20 for a season. In the nineteenth century, however, the river had literally dozens of famous salmon pools, for example in the fast-flowing waters near Stonebyres Falls. Salmon had disappeared from the Clyde, from above the Leven at any rate, by about 1900, but the long-term decline after 1945 of heavy industry and more recent improvements in the treatments of effluents have resulted in the return of salmon to the lower Clyde during the late 1970s and 1980s. A number of salmon were noted, for example, at Blantyre Weir in July 1988. It will, no doubt, be possible over the years to bring salmon back to the upper river by investing in expensive hatcheries, in salmon ladders at the various Falls of Clyde barriers, and in maturing tanks, for example in the old gravel pits at Roberton or Lamington. Permits for salmon fishing could easily even at current prices be £30 or £40 per person per day, so it is at last open to doubt whether this could be happily combined with the relatively open access for trout fishermen paying very different fees and possibly with quite different attitudes and outlooks. Unfortunately in the real world salmon might also mean importing new controlling mechanisms involving ghillies, bailiffs, and an active police presence to prevent city-based professional thieves and gangsters, who belong more to the world of Al Capone than John Buchan, from engaging in poaching raids which would not be remotely romantic.

Sources

There is something very romantic, very elegant, even very sensible in the idea of a river having a specific source, a pool, a spring, a well, a waterfall. The Tweed has its 'source' at the Tweed's Well east of the A701 south of Tweedhopefoot. The Aberdeenshire Dee 'starts' at the Wells of Dee, three springs on the Braeriach plateau. The Clyde is quite different. It 'emerges' as the river only where the Daer Water, the main stream, is joined by the Clydes Burn near Crookedstane farm south of Elvanfoot.

The name of the Clyde clearly 'flows' in a sense with and from the Clydes Burn (A), which just before Little Clyde farm divides into the Upper Moss Cleuch and the Lang Cleuch, the latter coming down from Tippet Hill at about 1400'. There is a second Clydes Burn (B) coming from Clyde Law at about 1550', but it runs into the Evan Water, a tributary of the river Annan. Both Clydes Burns run through the Roman camp at Little Clyde. Until the coming of the railway about a century and a half ago the Clydes Burn (B) ran north-west into the Clydes Burn (A). To prevent flood damage to the railway line a new mile-long channel including an aqueduct was prepared for the Clydes Burn (B), which transferred it permanently to the Evan Water.

The old Clydes Burn was then more impressive than the present wee trickle of water, but it must still have carried a smaller volume of water than the Daer. Did the name, Clwyd or the (Roman) Clotta or Clyde, follow over hundreds of years the lesser water course because the main Roman road south also ran roughly in this direction, more or less parallel to the present A74, whereas the Daer Water is on the line of the less important Roman road south-west towards Durisdeer by the A702? Did it all depend on a precedent fixed for political reasons?

The main stream is now certainly the Daer Water which comes from the north-eastern side of Gana Hill at about 1500'. It runs into and out of the Daer Reservoir, a total of some ten miles in all north to Watermeetings, where it is joined by the Potrail (Powtrail) Water. The Potrail comes some seven miles from Little Scawd Law north-east of Durisdeer.

Hyndford Bridge from the south-west.

One remarkable feature in this area is the close proximity of the watersheds of the rivers Clyde, Tweed, Annan and Nith. The old rhyme that

Annan, Tweed and Clyde
Rise a' oot o' ae hill side.

is a myth, but it is one of those popular fancies that conceals a useful lesson in geography. In the north the Clyde and the Daer, Potrail and Duneaton Waters and the upper stretches of the Tweed are slow, gently flowing streams. To the south, in contrast, the Evan Water and the Annan, and the Carron, Mennock and Crawick Waters going into the Nith, are much faster, rougher, rushing, aggressive streams cutting back into the watersheds of the Tweed and the Clyde. The Evan Water has 'captured' a series of one time Clydes Burn tributaries; the Crawick has cut deeply into the Duneaton Water basin to take over the Spango and the Wanlock Waters; the Mennock is on the move north as well. In all the Annan and the Nith have grabbed perhaps some fifty square miles of the original Clyde and Tweed basins.

Unaware of these transgressions the Clyde meanders peacefully on from Elavanfoot towards Crawford and Coulter and round Tinto to Thankerton, where it is about 655′ above sea level. On the way it has collected on the west the Elvan Water from the Lowther Hills, the Glengonnar Water from near Leadhills, the Duneaton Water from near the Ayrshire border, the Roberton Burn, and the Garf Water from north of Lamington; and on the east the Midlock Water and the Camps Water at Crawford , the Wandel Burn, and the Culter Water from Culter Waterhead Reservoir and Glenwhappen Rig south of Culter Fell.

In this peaceful and even sedate progress the river imperceptibly crosses the Southern Upland Fault line running south-west from St. Abb's Head by Coulter and Lamington and Crawfordjohn. To the north is the Midland Valley or Central or Lowland Plain and to the south the Southern Uplands. On the north and west the land has sunk down and the rocks of the Old Red Sandstone system are level with the older Ordovician rocks to the south and east. The Old Red Sandstone projects northwards as far as Crossford. At Cartland Craigs and the Falls of Clyde the Mouse and the Clyde have cut through the layers of glacial deposits and less resistant Carboniferous sandstones to the Old Red Sandstone.

Water for the People

The story of the reservoirs holding the water supplies for the people of Lanarkshire, the teeming multitudes of Hamilton, Motherwell, Airdrie, Lanark and East Kilbride, is in some respects quite extraordinary, in particular the way in which narrow-gauge railway lines were used to bring in supplies and materials. Daer, built between 1948 and 1954, lacks that element of steamy romance, but it is with a capacity of 5,300 million gallons of water by far the largest. The scale, the statistics are impressive. The enormous earthwork embankment and concrete wall is 2600′ long and stands 135′ high above the stream bed below.

Camps Reservoir took fourteen years from 1916 to 1930 to complete. Building materials, supplies and machinery were brought up from the main line at Crawford by a narrow-gauge railway laid between 1916 and 1919. German prisoners-of-war, over 200 at one time, formed the main labour force for work on the track. Both Daer and Camps were built for Lanarkshire County Council.

Culter Waterhead Reservoir was built between 1903 and 1907

Stonebyres Falls, in a T. Allom print published in London in 1835.

by the famous Glasgow firm of Robert McAlpine and Sons for the Motherwell New Water Works company. A 3′ narrow-gauge track was laid from the Caledonian Railway Symington-Peebles branch line at Causewayend just outside Biggar. The steam locomotives and rolling stock actually ran on the public road to Coulter, then up to Culter Allers farm and right up to the site of the reservoir below Knock Hill. The temporary village with its huts and canteens and no doubt a few 'wild colonial boys' amongst the navvies had for a time something of a reputation for riotous behaviour and even the appearance of a gold-diggers camp. Walking up the road above Culter Water today it seems utterly bizarre to think of a railway line in this quiet little corner of the world, quite apart from the engineering problems involved in coping with the hills.

Earlier still the Cowgill Upper Reservoir west of Culter Waterhead was built between 1895 and 1899 for the Airdrie and Coatbridge Water Works company. Amazingly a 3′ narrow-gauge railway line was laid here, starting from the 'Black Hut' south of Windgill and going on to Cowgill Upper. The second Lower Reservoir was built between 1899 and 1903.

Further east and into the Borders the well-known Talla Railway on a 4½′ gauge was laid between 1895 and 1897. The track with quite substantial bridges ran for some eight miles from Broughton Station by Rachan, Woodend ('dismantled railway' marked on

9

the O.S. Landranger map Sheet 72), and Crook Inn to Victoria Lodge. The Talla Reservoir supplying water to Edinburgh was completed in 1905. Several sections of the line can still be readily identified from the A701.

Lastly the Lochlyoch and Cleuch Reservoirs were built in 1897 and 1904 respectively for the town of Lanark.

Flood Plains and Gorges

North of Coulter and Wolfclyde motte the Clyde meanders round the huge 2320' mass of Tinto in a convoluted, almost womblike pattern, first north-west to Thankerton and north towards Carstairs and then south-west to Hyndford Bridge. On the way it collects the Glade Burn at Thankerton and the Medwin Water from the South and North Medwins at the Meeting south-west of Carnwath.

Tinto Hill, the dominant landscape feature, is part of a sheet of igneous rock running as far east as Dolphinton. At Tinto the red felsite may be up to 3500' deep. The felsite is quarried for road surfacing material (the old red roads of Lanarkshire) and garden chippings. Cairngryffe quarry, which is approached either from the Pettinain side or from the A73 before Hyndford Bridge, is especially prominent when seen from the back road, the B7016, from Carnwath to Biggar or from the Thankerton-Pettinain road.

The A70 from Douglas and the A73 below Tinto and the A72 through Biggar carry a steady flow of fast-moving coal lorries from the record-breaking opencast coal mining operations at Dalquhandy west of Coalburn. Unfortunately the long-dismantled railway lines to Lesmahagow, Larkhall and Hamilton could not be revived to take this traffic. The drivers are skilled, hardy professionals; but the lorries, really not much more than anachronistic dinosaurs belonging to an outdated technology, are a menace, particularly between Symington and Wolfclyde.

Quarrying is still an important source of employment in the Upper Ward of Lanarkshire. There are immense quantities of sand and gravel glacial deposits in layers typically up to 20' thick in the river valleys and in the spectacular and suprising sandy esker ridges in the Carnwath-Carstairs area close to the A70. The sand and gravel pits near the Clyde at Hyndford and at Thankerton (the Tinto Sand and Gravel Company) and also near the Mouse

Water at Carstairs lend a certain lunar quality to the grey winter landscapes. The sand and gravel has various uses including road bottoming, making concrete and plastering.

It is interesting to drive or, better still, walk along the back road north of the Clyde from Thankerton to Cormiston, looking across to the old gravel pits on the other side of the river, and then on to Wolfclyde looking east through the famous flat 'Biggar Gap' valley. It is a neat thought how easy it would be by cutting through the layers of sand to redirect the Clyde at this point off to the east and into the Tweed. This was indeed probably the course the 'upper' Clyde once actually followed. The Mouse and the Dippool and the Medwin Waters, which now turn west into the 'lower' Clyde, originally went in the other direction into the 'upper' Clyde; and in turn the 'upper' Clyde entered the Tweed before it was 'captured' for the 'lower' Clyde just south-west of Biggar. The Biggar Gap was filled up with glacial deposits long after these changes had taken place. Even today, however, the Biggar Water, which is a tributary of the Tweed near Broughton, when in flood takes water that should go to the Clyde off east to the North Sea via the Tweed.

After Hyndford Bridge the Clyde continues smoothly southwest until, after recruiting the Douglas Water at Crookboat, it accelerates north into and over the famous Falls of Clyde, Bonnington Linn, the 90' drop at Corra Lin, Dundaff Linn and Stonebyres Falls. The river falls some 230' over just under four miles, from 400' at Bonnington Linn to 170' after Stonebyres. The Clyde and its tributary at Kirkfieldbank, the Mouse Water, have cut right through to the Old Red Sandstone. The 100' deep gorges have a truly Gothic intensity and glamour. The steep sides at the Falls and at Cartland Crags and the terraced hillsides by Nemphlar and Hazelbank and Crossford and Rosebank provide the shelter for rich woodland vegetation and the famous orchards and market gardens. The Nethan at Crossford also cuts through a deep ravine below Craignethan Castle and down to the Clyde.

The Commercial River

The river from Crossford by Garrion Bridge to Cambusnethan passes through the last of the 'orchard country' up the Clyde and the last open farmland before it becomes, in the old phrase, the 'scullery maid for Motherwell and Glasgow'. Between Hamilton

Dumbarton Castle, in a print published in London in 1777 based on drawing in 1754 by Paul Sandby (1730-1809).

and Motherwell it is joined by the Avon Water after its journey north by Strathaven and Stonehouse to the spectacular gorges at Hamilton High Parks and Cadzow in Chatelherault Country Park.

It is easy nowadays amidst all the country parks and artificial lochs to forget the extent to which the whole economy in the area and the growth of the Lanarkshire towns and of the city of Glasgow depended in the nineteenth century on much harsher and more brutal realities, on the exploitation of mineral deposits and in particular on coal mining. The once vast Lanarkshire coalfield – 257 collieries in 1895, 210 in 1920 – ran from Glasgow to Airdrie and Coatbridge, to Blantyre and Motherwell on the north of the river, and to Cambuslang, Hamilton and Lesmahagow on the other side.

From Motherwell and Bothwell to Rutherglen and Glasgow the Clyde serviced the great industries, the iron and steel works and factories, and, after Rutherglen, the first shipbuilding and repair yards. It also became a roadway itself for boats coming and going with raw materials and manufactured goods. On the way it gathers in from the east and north-east the waters of the South Calder, just north of Motherwell, and the North Calder, just round the bend from Uddingston; and from the south the Rotten Calder, which runs north from the area above East Kilbride.

Glasgow sits on a series of glacial raised beaches and drumlin

Greenock c.1820 in a print by John H. Clark (1771-1863) in a series of his *Views in Scotland* published in London in 1824. Note the artist with pupils in the foreground looking over the merchants' houses to the busy shipbuilding yards below.

hills, for example at Gilmorehill and Hillhead. The Clyde, tidal up to Glasgow, collects the Kelvin just opposite Govan. The Kelvin comes down through the West End and then from the north-east by Kilsyth, Torrance, Balmore and Bardowie.

West of Govan and Linthouse the Clyde collects the White Cart and the Black Cart at Renfrew. Now on the whole most of the Clyde family of tributaries are well-behaved, douce children, but if there is one problem child in every family it is certainly the White Cart which, with its own tributary the Levern Water, is thoroughly unreliable, rude and unpredictable. It has a dreadful record of bursting its banks and flooding shops and homes in Stamperland, Cathcart, Battlefield, Shawlands and Pollokshaws. The Clyde River Purification Board operates a flood warning system, but the problem is perhaps more fundamentally that some houses are in places which no eighteenth or even nineteenth century landowner or surveyor would have considered appropriate.

The White Cart runs from the hills south-east of Eaglesham through Clarkston, Cathcart, Pollok, Paisley and Renfrew. It is joined at Crookston by the Levern Water which comes through

13

Neilston and Barrhead. The Black Cart comes in from Loch-winnoch and Johnstone to join the White Cart at the edge of Glasgow Airport (just at the moment incoming passengers are thinking of loosening their seat belts). Its tributary, the Gryfe, runs east from the Gryfe Reservoir in the hills behind Port Glasgow via Bridge of Weir and Houston.

On the other side of the river the Forth and Clyde Canal reaches the Clyde at Bowling and the River Leven joins it at Dumbarton. The lava uplands, the Kilpatrick Hills to the east, and the great volcanic rock on which Dumbarton Castle stands form a dramatic backcloth as the commercial river becomes the Firth of Clyde.

The Clyde from Glasgow and Govan to Dumbarton and Green-ock had become a major centre for shipping and shipbuilding by the third quarter of the nineteenth century, but this was no easy success story. Glasgow merchants and shipowners had to exercise vast amounts of patience and ingenuity, of money, sweat and tears, to clear the river channel of its islands and sandbanks, trap dykes and rocky reefs, particularly at Dumbuck ford near Dumbarton where the low water depth was only 2' in the 1760s. In the seventeenth and eighteenth centuries Glasgow merchants had to depend on the out-ports at Port Glasgow and Greenock. The Clyde at Glasgow in 1755 held only 3'8" of water at high and 15" at low water. The first effective dredging to clear sand and shingle began in the 1740s; the rocks at Dumbuck were removed after the second Act of Parliament in 1759; and improvements after further Acts in 1809, 1825, 1840 and 1858 opened up the Clyde as a highway for the world's shipping.

CHAPTER 2

Hunters, Farmers, Warriors:
Saints, Sinners and Improvers

Discovering the river Clyde in terms of human history means looking for the remains of the cultures and settlements of hunters and farmers and warriors and their descendants over some 9,000 years. The upper and lower Clyde shared the series of cultures referred to as Mesolithic, Neolithic, Bronze Age, Iron Age, Dark Age, Mediaeval and Modern common to the rest of Scotland and northern England. These cultures to some extent co-existed across the traditional and neat but misleading time periods usually awarded to them as a guide to understanding the past.

The first fully human men and women, as compared to the man-like creatures or *similitudines homines* of 250,000 to 200,000 BC, were living in southern Britain some 40,000 to 30,000 years ago. Possibly the first men to follow the Clyde were members of hunting parties visiting as summer migrants, or 'tourists', some time after the north of England was free of ice about 13,000 years ago. The ice sheet over southern Scotland melted away towards 8000 BC and a damp and warm climate followed. The land was covered with great forests and swamps and heavy dense vegetation.

Hunters

The first permanent residents along the Clyde were the Mesolithic nomadic hunters and fishers and food-gatherers driven by man's sense of adventure and curiosity to explore and discover new lands between 6500 and 4000 or 3500 BC. They may have stayed in one place for a few months or years in little groups of five or ten people. The overall number of people in the upper and lower Clyde was probably not much more at any one time than the number of players and supporters at a 1991 Scottish Second Division football match between Albion Rovers and Queen of the South.

Some of their camps may have been essentially hunting bases, some industrial sites where flint and chert scrapers and blades and arrows and axes were made, and others more long-term

15

stopping places with lightly-built huts in scooped hollows.

The first hunters probably came to the upper Clyde following the Tweed from the east and up the Annan and Nith from the Solway. Others would have followed the Ayrshire and Renfrewshire coastline to the Firth of Clyde and the lower river east of the Howe of Glasgow. The line between the sea and the land at different times was either below the present level or up to twenty-five or thirty feet above it.

One important workshop site was found on the north side of Woodend Loch near Coatbridge. Camps and settlement sites have been found on farmland along the Clyde between Crawford and Lanark, for example at Annieston and Quothquan Law near Thankerton and at Eastfield near Pettinain.

Mesolithic sites on eroded terraces and river haughs are not remotely dramatic, but it is worth looking out for tools and chippings coming out of old rabbit warrens, or 'bunnybanks' as the children call them, and mole hills.

Farmers

One major problem in comparing the history of the upper and lower Clyde is that evidence for prehistoric settlement in the Hamilton, Motherwell, Glasgow area is conspicuously thin. It would probably, however, be unwise to assume that Neolithic and Bronze Age peoples did not settle in strength along the lower Clyde, at least in the area east of Dumbarton. The problem, of course, is that industrialisation and urbanisation may have simply obliterated any traces of early sites. In contrast the Biggar, Carnwath, Elvanfoot area in the upper Clyde has an abundance of examples of early settlement, albeit without really having on show any of the more obviously spectacular and readily accessible Neolithic and Bronze Age sites found in Orkney and Argyll and Galloway.

The Neolithic world (4200 or 4000 to 2500 BC) and the Bronze Age (2500 or 2300 to 700 or 500BC) are perhaps best seen as one long period of the growth and development of a mixed farming economy which contained within it a series of overlapping cultures. These involved changes in belief and ritual, for example in burial practices including inhumation and cremation, changes in pottery styles and techniques variously associated with Beaker people, about 2000 BC, and Food Vessel people, and the

A yellow sandstone distance slab of the XX Legion found in 1969 on the Antonine Wall at the west end of Hutcheson Hill and now in the Hunterian Museum in the University of Glasgow. Note in the central triumphal arch the Roman standard-bearer holding the legionary eagle and on his right a goddess or deified empress. The vivid carving of the two captured tribesmen is probably the earliest record of people living along the river Clyde.

introduction from about 2000 BC of metal working in copper and gold and then bronze.

The number of farmers settling along the Clyde was almost certainly initially quite small. Perhaps we should allow for twenty to fifty persons for each major cairn and ritual site. The new people probably fused ultimately with the old nomadic folk to form a larger and healthier gene pool. The old view, anyway, of a series of wholesale immigrations by 'peoples' now seems less likely than a pattern of slow indigenous population growth with the occasional appearance of new ideas and new settlers. The average life span was about twenty-five to thirty years, and a man or woman of fifty was then very old.

The key to this world and what made a 'civilised' life possible was control of the environment, clearing woodland areas using stone axes or by large-scale burning, bringing land under cultivation with cereal crops, and grazing cattle and sheep and pigs and goats. What is really surprising and humbling is how over the centuries fields were cleared and settlements established in hill and moorland terrain up to 700 or 900 or even over 1200 feet in places later covered with peat and where mixed farming to-day would be difficult and certainly not financially viable. One factor that made this possible was the in general warmer and gentler climatic conditions between 2000 and 1000 BC. It was not, however, all a simple story. The virtual 'nuclear winter' between about 1170 and 1150 BC, resulting from volcanic activity in Iceland, was probably a major crisis in human history.

The great Neolithic buildings, the long cairns or communal tombs used as burial places and centres of activity for communities over periods of 1,500 or 2,000 years, are represented only by the modest remains at Burngrange near the Westruther Burn northeast of Carnwath and at Greens Moor above the South Medwin Water north-east of Dunsyre Hill. Neolithic implements and objects include stone axes from the Lamington, Biggar and Carnwath areas and a carved stone ball from Biggar Shiel.

For the Bronze Age along the upper Clyde there is a plethora of riches, although many sites are perhaps for the specialist prehistorian rather than the casual interested amateur. There are enormous numbers of round cairns of from 20 to 50 to 100 feet in diameter, generally covering box-like cist burials rather than enclosing chambers as in Neolithic long cairns. The most obvious and by far the most spectacular is the great cairn on the top of Tinto, no doubt located there just precisely so that it would, like an Ely or a Durham Cathedral, be seen from far away across the Clyde valley. Others include the Hero's Cairn on Swaites Hill north of the A73 and east of Cairngryffe, cairns on Kersewell Mains and south-east of Corse Law, both north-east of Carnwath, two cairns on Black Hill east of Crawfordjohn mill, and a round cairn with kerbstones at the Iron Age hill fort at Black Hill south of the A744 near Lesmahagow. There are also barrows at the Crawfordjohn Black Hill and the site of a barrow on Lanark Racecourse now only visible as a crop mark on aerial photographs.

There are also a number of cairnfields on hill and moorland sites up to 1,000 feet in the upper Clyde. These are in groups of ten, twenty, fifty, even two hundred small 10- to 20-feet diameter cairns. Some of the main concentrations, on Hare Law, Horse Law, Cairn Knowe, and Swaites Hill are in the Carnwath and Dunsyre area near the Medwin Waters and the Westruther Burn and between Pettinain and Thankerton. Bronze Age cists have been found in sand quarrying operations, for example at Patrickholm south-west of Larkhall on the west side of the Avon and at Boatbridge neat Thankerton, and rescue archaeology work in 1990 in advance of forestry development on Biggar Common hill near Quothquan has revealed early Bronze Age burials of some 3,500 years ago. Another type of site is the enclosed cremation cemetery, including one excavated example at Fall Hill near the Camps Water north of Crawford.

The more obviously spectacular ritual sites, stone circles, alignments of standing stones, and henges are modestly represented. There are two henges, one at Weston above the South Medwin east of Carnwath, and the other at Normangill, where the road, formerly the railway track from Crawford to Camps reservoir, runs right through the oval banks and ditches. The very large sixteen-acre enclosure near Blackshouse Burn on open ground north-west of Thankerton was perhaps a regional gathering place for farmers, herdsmen, metal workers and dealers to meet on special occasions. Some quite exquisite and sophisticated metal objects exchanged or sold or made locally have survived. These include the beautiful gold lunula from Coulter and a delicate gold lock-ring found at Boghall near Biggar Water. Recent 1990 survey work by local archaeologists and the Biggar Museum Trust on the line of the new M74 motorway north of Abington has produced evidence of more cairnfields and, remarkably, a previously unrecorded stone circle complex with perhaps twenty-three stones on the east side of the Wildshaw Burn (NS 882271).

There is a massive preponderance then of Neolithic and Bronze Age sites in the upper Clyde, first along a west-east axis from Carnwath and Dunsyre towards Dolphinton and the Pentlands, suggesting a prehistoric track along the hills north of the swamps and marshes in the Biggar Gap, and second further south along the Clyde which itself was an access routeway north and south. This is further confirmed by the evidence of surviving prehistoric field systems and settlements, for example at Ellershie

The Govan stone coffin and two hogbacks (all three were about 6 feet long) in John Stuart's *The Sculptured Stones of Scotland* published by the Spalding Club in Aberdeen in 1856.

Hill, Crookedstane, Normangill Rig and Bodsberry Hill near Crawford, and Black Hill near Crawfordjohn. It is fair to add that some of these are probably a record also of the life and work of later Iron Age farmers.

Warriors: Britons and Romans

By between 900 and 700 BC the farmers had to become warriors and military engineers. This was the result of a combination of pressures, population growth, land exhaustion, wetter and colder climatic conditions in which peat bogs covered areas previously worked and occupied, *and* because of the arrival of new settlers from South Britain. By about 700 BC and over the next six or seven centuries Celtic, that is British, 'Iron Age' bands, refugees, broken tribes, whole peoples, established themselves as the new masters. The old farming folk may have been slaughtered or enslaved like American Indians or merely absorbed. New ways and a new language, more akin to Welsh than to Gaelic, became dominant.

The tribes were seen by the Romans as grouped in 'federations'. It is not clear how far the Selgovae in Dumfries-shire and Peebles-shire extended their hegemony north and west into the upper Clyde and how much 'belonged' in the Iron Age to the Damonii in Ayrshire and Renfrewshire and the lower Clyde. The heavy concentration of forts in the upper Clyde might suggest that it was vulnerable and disputed territory. Did the forts around Lesmahagow and Quothquan belong to the Damonii and those around Coulter and Crawford to the Selgovae? Were frontiers and boundaries rather so flexible that there was no permanent dividing line?

For a thousand years or more wars and raids and conflict were the norm. Safety lay behind stockaded enclosures and in hill forts, promontory forts and crannogs. The people who lived along the Clyde then were magnificent savages, men to whom war was a game, an art and a science, who charged into battle mad from drugs and with hair stiffened straight with red lime and to the sound of war horns and trumpets. The women fought alongside the men in war groups, 'Boudiccas' from Biggar and 'Boadicias' from Broughton. They were also patrons of workshops producing elaborate decorated helmets and shields and sword hilts and richly enamelled jewellery, torcs, neck rings, hand mirrors, plaques.

Their religious specialists offered a variety of deities, gods associated with underground springs, pools, wells, lochs, rivers and streams: gods and goddesses of war and monster gods encouraging torture, such as divining by studying the death throes of ritual victims, human sacrifice, and hunting and collecting severed human heads: and animal deities, the great horned or antlered god, and the cult animals venerated by particular tribes, the horse, the bear, the wolf, the eagle, the serpent. The little bronze horse figurine from Birkwood near Lesmahagow and the bronze bull from Bank farm near Dolphinton perhaps belong to this category.

The hill forts along the Clyde are an extraordinary record of this warlike society. Some, for example, Arbory Hill at 1407' near Abington, are by any standard spectacular sites. Many were small forts for a local farming community; others, for example, Black Hill, Lesmahagow, covering four acres, were secure places and strengths for a much larger area. The defence lines are oval or sub-circular with single or multiple ditches and banks, occasionally with annexes or clear evidence of house sites or adjacent field systems. In some, for example, Cow Castle, the very complex defences were clearly altered and developed several times over hundreds of years.

The most southerly Clyde group includes Bodsberry Hill near Elvanfoot, the Berries Burn and Castle Hill forts near Crawford and Camps Knowe fort beyond the reservoir, Arbory Hill, Black Hill fort near Crawfordjohn, and Devonshaw Hill north of Wandel. Settlement or homestead sites include Ellershie Hill (955194) and Richie Ferry (945215) near Crawford, and Cold Chapel north of Abington.

The remarkable group near Coulter includes forts at Culter Park Hill, Snaip Hill, Cow Castle, White Hill, Mitchelhill Rings, and Nisbet and Langloch Knowe south and east respectively of Nisbet farm. There are also settlement sites on Nisbet and Snaip Hill, the site of a crannog at Green Knowe north-east of Coulter Shaw, and Iron Age or early mediaeval cultivation terraces on Culter Crags. The Dreva Craig fort above the Biggar Water and the Tweed near Broughton has a fine example of a *chevaux de frise*.

Beyond the Gap there are fort sites at Bizzyberry Hill and Toftcombs north-east of Biggar, Quothquan Law and Chester Hill near Thankerton, Whitecastle north of Shieldhill, Cocklaw south-west of Elsrickle, and at Fallburn on the north side of Tinto beside the track up to the summit.

Beyond Lanark again the picture is altogether more fragmentary. Note Black Hill fort (832435) between Kirkfieldbank and Lesmahagow, Double Dikes promontory fort north-east of Stonehouse on the Avon Water, a small fort in Chatelerhault Country Park, Dechmont Hill fort north-west of Blantyre, and then an enormous jump west to Walls Hill Fort in the Damonii heartland in Renfrewshire south of Johnstone and Elderslie. North of the Clyde Dumbarton Castle Rock should probably be regarded as a major Iron Age site.

The upper Clyde has still more riches to offer with a crannog at Hyndford near Lanark excavated in 1898, a souterrain or earth house at Wester Yardhouses near Carnwath excavated in 1923, and even a broch at Calla north of Carnwath first identified in 1952. The broch may perhaps be seen as an example of cooperation between men from the Western Isles or from Orkney or Caithness against the Roman invaders and slave gatherers at the end of the first century or early second century AD.

The local British tribes could not cope with the orderly tyranny of Rome, the sheer professionalism of the Roman army which had fought its way from the Euphrates to the Rhine and the

Danube and the Sahara. For a time the Clotta, the river and firth of Clyde, was to be the north-west frontier of the Empire.

The Roman invasions and direct imperial rule came in three phases. The first was the series of campaigns by Gaius Julius Agricola through Annandale and Clydesdale and central Scotland between AD 78 and 82. This was part of a grand strategy to conquer all of Britannia, England, Wales and Scotland, and probably also Ireland. It was followed by the Flavian occupation up to *c.* 105 with forts established in a line between probably Dumbarton (site unknown), Drumquhassle near Drymen, Bochastle, Doune and perhaps Stirling. The army then retreated to the north of England to the frontier line of Hadrian's Wall built in the 120s between the Tyne and the Solway.

In the second (Antonine) period from the early 140s southern Scotland was reoccupied and the Antonine Wall built between the Forth and the Clyde as a new linear barrier. This phase lasted into the 170s when the Wall and the forts along the Clyde and the Forth were finally abandoned.

Throughout the third period from *c.* 180 to 367 Hadrian's Wall marked the boundary of the Empire. There were some major campaigns, for example in 207–211 to Aberdeenshire; Birrens fort in Dumfries-shire was held to the end as a frontier outpost; and surveillance patrols and long-distance punitive strikes were mounted against dissident elements amongst the Selgovae and the Damonii. The Selgovae were probably treated as a sort of client buffer state with bribes and profitable contracts for supplying the insatiable slave markets of Gaul and Rome.

The immediately visible record of the Roman forts and camps and roads along the Clyde is slight, but a glance at the Landranger O.S. maps reveals something of the sheer profusion of sites and routes over a wide area. Some were recorded and surveyed by William Roy in the 1750s and published posthumously in his *Military Antiquities of the Romans in Britain* in 1793, but most are known from aerial photographs taken in dry summer seasons when the lines of old walling and ramparts and roads and ditches and pits can be traced.

The main road for the first and second class postal services, for wagon supply trains and for troop movements from Dover and London and York to the edge of 'civilisation' at Old Kilpatrick near the Dumbuck Ford ran close to the line of the A(M)74 at

Beattock. It continued north by Auldhousehill, Errickstane Hill, Beattock Summit and Little Clyde to Bodsberry Hill at Elvanfoot; then still along the east bank of the river to Crawford fort, a zigzag over Raggengill Hill Pass to Cold Chapel, and hence to Wandel, Lamington, Coulter, Springfield, Causewayend and Biggar; and by Candy Mill and the A702 to Slipperfield Loch and Carlops, and hence to the Forth. Another road, not as yet located, probably followed the Clyde by Thankerton to Castledykes fort between Carstairs and Lanark, and hence by Cleghorn, Kilncadzow and Yieldshields and the line of the A721 to Wishaw, and hence to Bothwellhaugh fort and to Balmuildy on the Antonine Wall between Bearsden and Kirkintilloch.

The other road north from Dalswinton or Carzield and from Drumlanrig in Nithsdale ran through Durisdeer and east of Well Hill beside the Potrail Water to the Cleuch Burn, and then by the A702 by Nether Fingland to a bridge over the Clyde near Elvanfoot.

A cross-country route from Newstead near Melrose ran west from Lyne and Harecairn near Elsrickle to cross the North Medwin near Carnwath Mill and hence by Lampits to Castledykes. It probably continued west by the Mouse Water or Lanark to Kirkfieldbank, Stonebyres and Corramill to Dykehead south of Stonehouse towards Loudon Hill fort and the Ayrshire coast near Irvine. Sea routes were important: the Roman navy with bases in the Firth of Clyde supplied the army on the Antonine Wall and Renfrewshire, and probably also the forts in the lower Clyde from Rutherglen.

Surviving road sections and quarry pits are generally not easy to recognise. The best are the road along the Potrail Water from Durisdeer and the sections over Raggengill Hill, in Collielaw Wood north of Cleghorn, and near the A702 south of Elvanfoot. The possible road link from Castledykes south to Crawford by Carmichael Hill, Howgate Mouth, Limefield and Roberton is at best left 'not proven'.

The least permanent fortifications were the marching camps for armies of 5,000 or 10,000 men. Examples, nearly all close to the Clyde, include the 21-acre camp at Little Clyde, where parts of the north rampart and ditch can still be seen; two camps at Crawford, south-east of the village; Wandel; the 40-acre camp at Lamington with the parish church near the centre; Cornhill, near Coulter between Culter House and the Castle Plantation; a 30-acre camp near Carstairs identified in 1989; a 106-acre camp at Spittal near Carnwath; a 42-acre camp west of Corbiehall near Castledykes; the camp at Cleghorn surveyed by General Roy with clear earthworks still in Camp Wood; and, another recent discovery, a 20-acre camp south of the Avon near Strathaven. Camps and forts are uniformly rectangular with rounded corners and single or multiple banks and ditches.

Permanent forts include Crawford (954214), a 2-acre site north-west of Castle Crawford and between the Camps Water and the Berries Burn, the large regional headquarters at Castledykes (928442) south-east of Corbiehall, and the 4-acre fort at Bothwellhaugh (731578) beside the South Calder Water in Strathclyde Country Park. The Flavian fort at Barochan Hill north of Houston and the Antonine fort at Whitemoss north-west of Bishopton, both in Renfrewshire, were clearly bases for controlling the Dumbuck Ford and the Firth of Clyde.

Fortlets for garrisons of 50 to 100 men, part of a tightly organised system of surveillance and control, include Redshaw Burn (030139), Wandel, and Lurg Moor in Renfrewshire south-west of the B788 and Port Glasgow, and Outerwards on the road from Largs north-east to Loch Thom. A signal station site at Raecleuch or White Type south-west of the Devil's Beef Tub on the A701 and a watch tower site (999153) under the forest near Beattock Summit are examples of the many smaller structures still to be discovered.

North of the Clyde the Antonine Wall was another remarkable demonstration of imperial power. It was in no sense an Iron Curtain or a Maginot Line behind which the army waited passively to be attacked. The whole point of the 37-mile long wall and the forts and fortlets along it was to establish a sound base for fast mobile patrols mounting immediate retaliatory strikes against raiders. Very little survives of the forts at Old Kirkpatrick, Duntocher and Castlehill at the west end of the Wall. The distance slabs and altars in the Hunterian Museum in the University of Glasgow are, however, dramatic evidence of Roman rule and power.

Saints and Sinners (367 to 1735)

After the collapse of Roman power in Britain the political

history of the upper and lower Clyde is in a sense straightforward: it became part of the British kingdom of Strathclyde which had emerged by the early 400s with Alcuith or Dumbarton Castle Rock as its capital. This Strathclyde, including Dunbartonshire, Renfrewshire, Ayrshire, Lanarkshire and parts of Stirlingshire, survived until the death of its last king, Owen, in 1015. This neat summary, however, conceals a much more complex and chaotic history. 'National' boundaries were continually changing. The only safety and security lay behind the defences of the old hill forts and strengths. The Gaelic-speaking Scotti in the kingdom of Dalriada in the west and the Picti in northern and eastern Scotland were a persistent threat; and the Anglian hordes in Bernicia or Northumbria had established their supremacy in Dumfries and Galloway and had taken over eastern Scotland as far north as Edinburgh and Stirling by the 640s. The Picts and Scots were still more dangerous after they were united under Kenneth, son of Alpin, in 843. The Norsemen and Gall-Ghaidhil from Ireland and the Hebrides and the Isle of Man had established themselves in Arran and probably along the Ayrshire coast by the early tenth century: Dumbarton indeed was lost for a time after being captured in 870 after a long siege. Still somehow Strathclyde survived as an independent kingdom until in 1015 Malcolm II became king of the Scots and Picts and Britons. After the battle of Carham in 1018 he finally incorporated the Lothians in 'Scotland'.

One important element sustaining the kingdom of Strathclyde was the long established tradition of control from the centre which the Christian church provided. It is highly likely that Christianity spread north along the Clyde and Tweed from Carlisle and from St Ninian's diocese at Whithorn in the late fourth and fifth centuries. Glasgow, with the church founded by St Conthigirnus or St Kentigern in the late sixth century, Dumbarton, Govan and Inchinnan with their churches dedicated to St Constantine and St Conval respectively, and Hamilton Low Parks or Cadzow are early church sites in the lower Clyde. Lanark, Biggar, Lamington and Crawford are possible but uncertain sites in the upper Clyde. The diocese centred on Glasgow as the seat of the bishop for the kingdom of Strathclyde was probably organised into parishes during the sixth and seventh centuries.

The best, almost the only way of capturing something of the essence, of the spirit of the period, is to study the collection of tenth- and eleventh-century carved stones at Govan. Govan on the south bank of the Clyde was a key crossing point with stepping stones until 1768 and a ferry. The collection of twenty-six cross shafts and upright and recumbent slabs and hogbacks kept inside the church built by Robert Rowand Anderson in 1884–88 is quite unique. The 6-ft long stone coffin or sarcophagus with Pictish hunting scenes and animals and Anglian style interlace work is a wondrous thing to have survived so many centuries in such a busy place. The five $6^1/_2$- to $7^1/_2$-feet long hogback stones represent Danish/Norse/northern English bowlike shaped rectangular houses with wooden shingles or tiles. Note the carved roof ridges and beast terminals with crude jaws and legs. Other hogbacks can be seen at Luss and Dalserf. The shrine cover and cross at Inchinnan New Parish Church and the Netherton Cross at Hamilton also date to the tenth century.

The new kings of Scotland, in particular Malcolm Canmore's sons, David I (1124–53) and Malcolm IV (1153–65), began a revolutionary modernising programme with the introduction of the new feudal order into central and local government, in land tenure and in the church. The key to making this new order possible and permanent was the arrival of an élite of men expert in war and castle-building, men from Normandy and Brittany and Flanders and Poitou via Yorkshire and Cumbria, men hungry for land and power — the de Lindsays from Lincolnshire at Crawford, William de Somerville from Yorkshire at Carnwath or Libberton, Simon Loccard at The Lee north-west of Lanark, Robert Croc at Crookston south-west of Glasgow. The land grants they received, whether for old estates or for subdivisions of existing units, were based on knight service.

Some of their castles, for example Crookston, were timber structures built inside an oval or sub-circular ringwork with a simple bank and ditch and palisaded defences. Most in Lanarkshire were mottes, oval or rectangular or the classical Christmas pudding shape, circular mounds from 10 to 30 to 40 feet high, perhaps heightened several times over two hundred years, with a deep and wide ditch round the base. Some had a bailey or courtyard defended by an outer ditch and stockade. On top of the mound, or built into it, was a wooden blockhouse or tower, crenellated, perhaps with external fighting platforms as shown in the Bayeux Tapestry. Access to the top of the motte was by a flying bridge over the ditch or by steps up the side of the mound from a bridge over the ditch below. The best example in the area is the exceptionally steep motte on the golf course at Carnwath.

Baldwin of Biggar was the leader of a group of Flemings introduced by David I or Malcolm IV in the 1150s or 1160s to carve out new estates for themselves between Abington and Pettinain. Their castles along the Clyde include the motte and bailey north of Abington in Crawfordjohn parish held by Baldwin's stepson, John: the motte at Moat in Roberton parish which, when excavated in 1979, turned out to be late thirteenth or fourteenth century — the twelfth-century site was possibly at Castledykes just west of the village on the north bank of the Roberton Burn; the small Wolfclyde motte north of Coulter; and the large motte and bailey in Biggar where the B7016 joins the A702. The promontory site on the Clyde at Bower of Wandel may have been the location of the twelfth-century castle for Wandel parish; and the moated manor earthworks at Covington may be the remains of twelfth- or thirteenth-century defences. In the lower Clyde the motte at Hamilton (726566) close to the M74 is one of the few surviving examples.

Baldwin of Biggar, who also held Houston and Inverkip in Renfrewshire, was the sheriff of Lanark or Clydesdale. The establishment of the new royal sheriffdom and the foundation of the royal burghs at Lanark, Rutherglen and Renfrew, probably in the reign of David I in the 1140s or 1150s, were part of the vigorous reform programme which fixed patterns of government and economic growth for the future. The sheriffdom was split in 1402 between Lanark and Rutherglen, the Upper and Nether Wards.

In the church the new pattern of small parishes coincided with the landholdings along the Clyde. At a higher level the system of centralised territorial dioceses, rather akin to royal sheriffdoms, was revived and developed. Oddly the monastic and religious orders, busy, practical, orderly communities, centres for prayer and worship and contemplation and for practical creative work in land use and management, so prominent in the Borders and Galloway, were far less important in Lanarkshire. The

Bothwell Castle in a print published in 1775 based on a drawing by Paul Sandby c.1754. This is the best view, from the south-west, showing the round keep. Note the 'Palace' just above the trees in the distance on the right.

Tironensians from Kelso were brought to Lesmahagow by David I in 1144, the Augustinian canons from Jedburgh were established at Blantyre Priory some time before 1249, the Cistercians from Newbattle had a grange at Dunpelder or Drumpellier near Coatbridge, the Franciscans were settled at Lanark by Robert I in 1325/6, there were Dominicans in Glasgow before 1246 and Franciscans before 1473/6, and collegiate churches were founded in Bothwell in 1397/8, in Carnwath in 1424, in Hamilton in 1450/1 and in Biggar in 1545/6.

To most people a 'mediaeval' castle means a great stone keep or a courtyard castle with corner towers and a gatehouse. At Rutherglen, Renfrew, Dumbarton, Glasgow these have all disappeared, but Bothwell Castle on the Clyde near Uddingston is everything a great thirteenth-century castle should be with an enormous round keep or donjon and the planned layout of a very large courtyard castle. The history of the development of mediaeval military architecture in Scotland is completed with a good range of examples of the tower houses of greater and lesser families, from the scholarly, sophisticated sixteenth-century castle with artillery defences at Craignethan and the Renaissance elegance of Newark near Port Glasgow, to the smaller towers at Corra Castle, Castle Crawford, Covington and Hallbar near Carluke. The towers, of course, were not single buildings standing in isolation, but part of complexes of farm buildings, stables, barns, retainers' quarters, all inside a stone barmkin wall.

The importance attached to security as opposed to comfort and elegance is a reflection of a number of problems, the weakness of central government in Scotland, the petty rivalries between neighbouring families, and the quarrels between rival varieties of the Christian religion after the Scottish Reformation in 1560 and throughout the seventeenth century. The sorrow and grief, the waste and slaughter in the struggles between Episcopalians and Presbyterians who were almost equally evangelical, fanatical and intolerant is an unedifying spectacle. No doubt many decent and sensible folk managed to live quiet lives by conforming to whatever was the prevalent fashion in the Presbyterian (1638-60 and after 1689) and Episcopalian (1660-89) periods of dominance. It is difficult today to appreciate fully the extent of the bigotry and arrogance of all parties in an era when the faithful were schooled to regard heretics and heathens and supporters of other churches as evil, as the devil's disciples. Christianity did not mean love, charity, tenderness, tolerance and benevolence, but the imposition of righteous certainties by doctrinaire intellectuals and busybodies. Far too much attention can be paid to the unseemly squabbles over essentially trivial issues and the atrocities committed by brave but foolishly naive Episcopalians and Covenanters alike. The real dangers in allowing evangelical zealots to control religious organisations is best seen by looking at the record of the Presbyterians and the Episcopalians in burning at least 2,500, possibly as many as 4,000 women and men as witches between the 1590s and the early 1700s. The last major burnings were in Renfrewshire in 1697.

The abolition in 1735 of the statutes dealing with witchcraft and the invention of tolerance as a virtue marked the triumph of common sense and expediency over the religious principles of Covenanters, Presbyterians and Episcopalians. Tolerance was imposed upon the Scottish people by the British government post-1707 and the Scottish aristocracy. It was part of a welcome retreat from the supernatural world and towards control of the environment through improvements in agriculture and technology and education. Until the eighteenth century life was seen essentially in terms of the passage of the soul through a bleak and brutal and transitory existence. During the eighteenth century men and women were allowed to display the courage of disbelief and to develop a healthier preoccupation with problems and conditions with which we are more familiar today: wages, debts, taxes, fraud, bankruptcies, employment and parliamentary elections.

Improvers

The eighteenth and early nineteenth century really was the 'Age of the Enlightenment'. A new confidence and optimism was evident at different levels of society. Much of the rural landscape which we see around us today was created at this time, the enclosed and improved fields, the planned estates with formal avenues and gatehouses and gardens and follies, the planned villages, the solid farmhouses. The hub of each of these enterprises was usually the great country house with rooms stuffed with landscapes by Jacob More and Alexander Nasmyth, portraits by Ramsay and Raeburn, and prints by Paul Sandby, William Daniell and John Clark. Many of the estates were purchased by successful Glasgow merchants and bankers with the money to spend on the new improvements and create an elegant and cultivated environment. The new roads with fast stage-coach services, the bridges over the Clyde, the Clydesholm Bridge at Kirkfieldbank, the Hyndford and Thankerton and Crossford and Garrion Bridges, the Cartland Bridge over the Mouse Water, the Forth and Clyde Canal, the new harbours and lighthouses, the deepened channel of the Clyde beyond Glasgow, all put together amount to a Transport Revolution.

The first Industrial Revolution from the 1750s to the 1830s was essentially a matter of using traditional water and wind and human power sources more effectively than ever before. It was a revolution based partly on agriculture with profits from the land invested in more and larger grain mills, tanneries and breweries; partly on the profitable development of trade and commerce between Glasgow and the Clyde and North American markets; and partly on textiles, lint mills, waulk mills, and the new and much larger cotton mill factories at, for example, New Lanark and Blantyre. Coal mined for domestic consumption brought enormous profits to some landowners, in particular the Dukes of Hamilton, and the first Lanarkshire ironworks (cast iron) were established at Wilsontown in 1781.

The second Industrial Revolution from the 1830s onwards was something on a totally different scale. The vast expansion of the Lanarkshire coal field, the (malleable) iron works (Motherwell, Mossend) from the 1840s, the steel foundries (Hallside, Clydebridge, Dalzell, Wishaw) from the 1870s and 1880s, shipbuilding at Govan and Port Glasgow and Greenock, railway engineering workshops, were all part of a whole cycle of massive and rapid economic growth. It is a now familiar story of the ruthless exploitation of finite mineral resources, vast profits and wealth unequally divided, conspicuous expenditure by successful industrialists and capitalists in their opulent piles and palaces, pollution, waste, a whole underworld of crime and poverty and prostitution and religious bigotry, ultimate decline and decay and degradation.

The second half of the nineteenth century was also the Railway Age, and what a network of train services there were in the Clyde area — Glasgow to Coatbridge and Airdrie in 1841, Glasgow to Carlisle in 1848, Rutherglen and Hamilton and Motherwell in 1849, Lanark in 1855, Hamilton to Larkhall and Auchenheath to Douglas in 1864, Symington to Biggar and Broughton in 1860, Carstairs to Dunsyre and Dolphinton to Leadburn in 1867, Elvanfoot to Leadhills in 1901. The growth of the railways made possible some dispersal of the urban masses from Glasgow out to the towns along the Firth of Clyde and also south to Lanark and Thankerton and Symington. Strange anomalies persisted right through the period however; for example, the ferry floats on the Clyde. As late as 1905 a new ferry float was ordered for the Lampits ferry across the Clyde near Carstairs.

By the late nineteenth century the Clyde was passing through almost two different countries, the south a world of rural values and country ways, the north beyond Dalserf a raucous, noisy melting pot for Highlanders, Lowlanders, Irish from the nine counties of Ulster, Jews, Italians, Poles, Lithuanians, Greeks, to be joined more recently by Pakistani, Gujerati, Bangladeshi, Sikh, Chinese and English immigrants. Dry population data for the number of people living in some of the parishes along the Clyde between 1801 and 1951 perhaps illustrates better than any

Garrion Mill in 1962.

words can the stark nature of the contrast between these two worlds.

Year	Wiston and Roberton	Biggar	Pettinain	Lanark
1801	757	1,216	430	4,692
1851	839	2,049	420	8,243
1901	412	1,897	271	8,103
1951	445	2,212	277	9,250

Year	Rutherglen	Blantyre	Bothwell	Motherwell and Dalzell
1801	2,437	1,751	3,017	611
1851	7,954	2,848	15,283	2,262
1901	21,011	14,145	45,904	37,257
1951	33,353	17,766	63,185	42,601

Year	Glasgow (c. 23,546 in 1755)
1801	77,385
1851	333,657
1901	761,709
1951	1,089,767

Since 1951 the population of Glasgow has fallen by about twenty-five per cent.

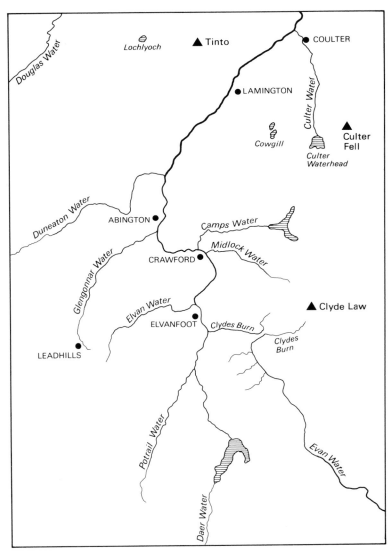

Sources of the Clyde to Coulter.

CHAPTER 3

Clydesmuir to Clydesdale: Elvanfoot, Crawford and Lamington

The overwhelming impression of the high country at and beyond the 'gathering of the waters' of the Clyde near Elvanfoot is of bare bleak moorland and dull rounded hills covered with peat and heather: nostalgically, romantically, a still dreamy quiet world; realistically, for most of the year a hard land on which to survive. James Maconchie, the parish minister at Crawford two hundred years ago, saw it as a 'naked' country where even in June water froze to ice a quarter of an inch thick.

It is very easy therefore to forget the extent to which these places were successfully farmed, fields cleared, crops grown and cattle grazed and overwintered in byres, not only in periods with relatively warmer climatic conditions, but also in the colder later sixteenth and seventeenth centuries. Recent work on seventeenth century wills and testaments and archaeological fieldwork by the Biggar Museum Trust has produced a totally new picture of the early farming economy of this hill country. The number of two storey fortified farmhouses or bastle houses is especially surprising and suggests the extent to which small lairds and tenant farmers still had to rely on stout walls and a strong right arm for security against raids and incursions by Johnstones or Douglases or Crichtons and probably also their more immediate neighbours and relatives. Important examples of bastles have been found as far north as Nemphlar, at Windgate in the hills south of Cowgill Reservoir, at Snar and Glendorch south-west of Crawfordjohn, and at Glenochar near the A702 south of Elvanfoot. A new site, Thorril Castle (865310), was located in 1990 on the M74 fieldwork project north of Abington.

Durisdeer to Elvanfoot

The best way to explore the upper reaches of the Potrail Water is to go by car or take the Edinburgh-Dumfries bus to the Durisdeer road end on the A702 and then walk north on the line of the Roman road between Durisdeer Hill and Well Hill to join the Southern Upland Way at Overfingland. The very well-

Discovering The River Clyde

preserved fortlet (902048) watching over the pass was part of a complex control and surveillance system. The bus from Elvanfoot through the Dalveen Pass can again be used to get back to a car left en route. The Roman road north of Watermeetings and Glenochar is best explored from Elvanfoot or from the Daer road end. Really keen walkers can join the Southern Upland way going either north-west by Lowther Hill to Wanlockhead or east from the Potrenick Burn to the Daer Reservoir.

The little church built in 1906 looking over the Clyde at Elvanfoot is now disused. The pulpit, communion table and some chairs made by local women at Lady Colebrooke's workshop at Glengonnar have been acquired by the Biggar Museum Trust. The stained glass includes a memorial to the actor Wilson Barrett from Stephen Adam's Glasgow studio.

On the opposite bank of the Clyde is Crookedstane, a 1000 acre hill farm with 530 Blackface ewes. It is also the home of the 'South Lanarkshire Llamas'. The gentle, rather aristocratic looking llamas are used as pack animals for trekking across the Border hills. White and brown in colour, four feet high at the shoulder, weighing up to 400 lbs., and thoroughly environmentally friendly (they do best on rough scrub vegetation), they are a spectacular and somehow very appropriate addition to local life. They blend into the bare, bleak hill country behind as if they belonged there.

At the moment of writing in February 1991 the A74 or M74 at Elvanfoot and further north between Abington and Douglas is in the middle of major reconstruction and realignment work. Quite apart from this temporary inconvenience the motorway between Elvanfoot and Beattock Summit is far too dangerous a road to encourage visitors to even contemplate slowing down or turning off to look for Roman roads or camps or fortlets, let alone the two Clydes Burns or forest tracks towards Clyde Law. Read about them as they used to be in the books by Neil Munro and Donald Maxwell but select other priorities.

From Elvanfoot (at 1000') follow the B7040 along the Elvan Water to Leadhills (1350'). The great eight arch concrete and brick Rispin Cleuch viaduct (901159) by Charles and Robert McAlpine and Sons for the Leadhills and Wanlockhead Light Railway (1901-38) is likely to be demolished by British Rail in 1991. The line joined the Caledonian Railway at Elvanfoot.

Crawfordjohn from the air with the B740 running through the village from the top right hand corner of the photograph. Note the castle site, the grassy hillock above the play area in the left centre, the Colebrooke Arms Inn below, and the T plan church to the left of the school.

The Leadhills area, of course, was an important centre of mining operations for gold and silver and lead from the thirteenth century. Gold workings ('Gold Scours', 'Gold formerly wrought here') are recorded along the Longcleuch Burn and the Shortcleuch Water. Note in Leadhills itself the (Allan Ramsay) Circulating Library founded in 1741 and Woodlands Hall, a small two storey house built for James Stirling c. 1733/34. The mines and the village were substantially re-equipped and rebuilt by the Leadhills Silver and Lead Mining and Smelting Company in 1876. Mining continued up to 1928.

Crawfordjohn

- or *Out of the World and into Crawfordjohn,* as 'they' say. The village really is a delightful surprise. Although only two miles by the B740 from the busy A74 or five miles from the A73 by Maidencote and Netherton, the green and fertile little hidden valley does seem like a different world. It is well worthwhile spending a day exploring the village or town (Crawfordjohn became a burgh of barony in 1668) and the surrounding countryside.

Park near the Colebrooke Arms Inn. The hillock opposite the inn and above the play area may be the site of a castle. There was another castle site at Boghouse just south-west of the village. Either may have been used by Sir James Hamilton of Finnart who resigned his land of Crawfordjohn to James V in 1535 in exchange for the barony of Kilmarnock.

The T plan church, built in 1817 on the site of an earlier, possibly twelfth century church, is likely to be open on Saturday and Sunday afternoons in the summer. It is now the centre of the Crawfordjohn Heritage Venture, a lively local history museum service. It has copies of local records and rentals, a detailed 1889 plan of the churchyard useful for family history researchers, costumes including a fine shepherd's plaid, records of the Free Church 1856-1929, photographs and plans of Gilkerscleuch House, log books and/or photographs of Whitecleuch and Auchendaff Schools, books from the Friendly Society Library (1799-1833) and Crawfordjohn Library, examples of rural crafts past and present, and an enthusiastic welcome.

As at Leadhills the area has an interesting industrial history, with the Craighead Quarry which was famous for its Essexite curling stones, lime works at Whitecleuch, and lead workings at Glendorch and Glendouran.

A good short walk capturing something of the flavour of the area is to take the minor road east above the Duneaton Water to Crawfordjohn-mill looking across to the fort and settlement and linear earthwork on Black Hill (908239 and 907241). Coming back to the car take the road from Balgray up to the B740 and hence down to the village.

Crawford and Abington

The Clyde at Crawford and Abington almost seems to be

squeezed between on the west the throbbing modern motorway between Scotland and England and on the east the old Caledonian Railway (now British Rail) line opened in 1848. There is a great deal to savour in this, the best of Clydesmuir, before the river flows into Clydesdale in the more open valley below Tinto. The best way to enjoy the area is to travel by bus to or park your car in Abington near the Royal Bank of Scotland or the Police Station. Take the road east across the railway line to Southwood. The Roman road round Raggengill Hill comes down to the line of the modern road just behind the farm dam and the Caravan Club Certificated Location.

Modestly fit walkers might tackle the stiffish climb up to the fort on Arbory Hill (1406') from Cold Chapel farm or from Raggengill Burn. The view from the fort up the Clyde is very worthwhile. The Iron Age fort has clearly defined double ramparts and ditches and banks and some hut foundations, and the remains of a field system and some cultivation ridges can be traced nearby.

A splendid winter or summer walk is to turn south at Southwood farm and continue on the minor road from which there is a unique view of the railway line a few feet away and the river below. The churchyard at Kirkton, probably the site of the early church dedicated to St. Constantine, is on the opposite bank of the river. Note the very narrow strip of land between Castle Hill and the river at the second railway bridge – vulnerability to ambush from above probably explains why the Roman road from Crawford went over Raggengill Hill. The complex Iron Age site at Ritchie Ferry (945215) on the left has one large single ramparted settlement with eight round houses and two separate small homesteads or settlements adjacent.

Continue on the same road to Castle Crawford or Tower Lindsay. The 20' high mound, probably twelfth-century motte, was held by the Lindsays, the Earls of Crawford, until 1488. The sixteenth- or seventeenth century buildings, the remains of a rather palatial residence, are now very dangerous and the precinct should be studied from the outside only. No traces remain of the two acre Roman fort which was on the open ground north and west of the castle. It was excavated in 1938 and between 1961 and 1966.

The road beyond the Castle Crawford along the Camps

The monument to Matthew McKendrick on top of the motte north of Abington just below the A73.

Water through the henge at Normangill is a fine long walk, with cremation cemeteries, early settlements and fort sites on Fall Hill and Normangill Rig and in Camp Knowe Wood. Walkers can return from Crawford to Abington using the Dumfries – Edinburgh bus service.

Attempts were made to establish Crawford as first an ecclesiastical burgh in 1242-49 and then as a burgh of barony in 1510-11, but the present village is primarily a nineteenth century resort based on access by passenger train from Glasgow and Edinburgh.

Abington was part of the large mediaeval parish of Crawfordjohn. The classical motte and bailey north of the village on the west bank of the Clyde opposite Cold Chapel can be viewed from the A73. The monument on the edge of the motte above the steep river bank is to Matthew McKendrick (1848-1926), the local postmaster, 'a worthy man and a fine fisher', an epitaph of which even John Buchan would have been proud. The monument was erected in recognition of his work in improving facilities for angling.

South of Abington the B797 is a very pleasant road running up through sheep country to Leadhills. Some mineralogical potential has been noted here in the past: the O.S. First Edition 6" scale map records 'Gold found here' at a site (about 925221) on the north bank of the Glengonnar Water just east of where it is joined by the Glencaple Burn.

Roberton and Wiston

From Abington the Clyde glides smoothly north between four small parishes, Roberton and Wiston on the west and Wandel and Lamington on the east, all the time closer to the brooding mass of Tinto. Robert's town, the 'villa Roberti', the town of Robert the brother of Lambin c. 1160, was probably the land from Duneaton Water to Dungavel Hill. His caput may have been at Castledykes above Roberton mill and church. The motte at Moat above the Clyde is a late thirteenth or fourteenth century site. The chapel was originally dependent on Wiston, but was a parish church from shortly before 1279 until 1772 when the two parishes were merged. The cluster of buildings round the now disused church (1891), the circular churchyard, the late eighteenth century corn mill and the lade system, the old school

42 *Discovering The River Clyde*

and the seventeenth century bridge make an interesting period group.

To explore the area park at the road end near the A73 or take the bus (the Dumfries – Edinburgh service goes past Roberton, Wiston and Lamington) to Roberton and walk up the road to Nap Bridge. The longer circuit round Dungavel Hill by Muirhead and Limefield and then east by Newton to Wiston Mains is an excellent walk.

Wiston, the 'villa Vicii', from Wice or Wicius is similar in many respects to Roberton. The church (1886) which has some good stained glass by Stephen Adam and Son of Glasgow (1893-1904) is set in another round churchyard on the hill above the Gart Water. To explore the area start from Millrig Road off the A73 north of Castledykes and walk along to the village. The road up the hill to the right goes past Wiston Lodge, a Y.M.C.A. residential centre, the road to the left down to the Old Corn Mill and across to Wiston Mains. Another short circuit is to take either road by Wiston Mains or Millrig to walk to Greenhill, the site of a seventeenth century laird's house now rebuilt in Biggar, and return to the village. For a long trek round Tinto take the B7055 and then the road north by Howgate Mouth and Howgate, and turn right across the Carmichael Burn and east by Lochlyoch, Woodend and Fallburn to the A73 where the buses from Biggar to Lanark run on a more or less hourly each way service.

The 110 acre Wyndales Farm on the A73 north of Wiston is likely to open shortly as a visitor centre or open farm. This will be the first of what will hopefully be a number of diversification proposals to emerge in the 1990s. Overnight accommodation is already available at several local farms, including Netherton, Craighead and Gilkerscleuch Mains near Crawfordjohn and Abington.

Wandel and Lamington

Wandel (Quendal) or Hartside parish, from William de Hertisheved c. 1225, has no village or cluster of houses and since the parish was merged with Lamington as far back as 1608 it is perhaps difficult to think of it now as a separate entity. It was important, however, in terms of communications and river crossings. The Roman road ran through the parish and there was a fortlet (944268) south-west of Wandel farm and a marching

The Bower of Wandel river promontory site with the remains of the Jardine's tower house. Note the Roberton Burn joining the Clyde from the west.

camp just to the south of it. Wandel Bridge built in 1683 was the crossing place over the Clyde for all the traffic, carts, wagons, pack horses going from Leadhills to Edinburgh.

The Jardines held land here from the twelfth to the seventeenth century and the Bower of Wandel on the river bend opposite Roberton was probably the site of their manor and tower house.

Lamington takes its name from Lambin Asa in the 1160s. The motte (992309) above the A702 may have been his caput. It may also have been associated with Hew Braidfute of Lamingtoune who in Blind Harry's poem was the father-in-law of William Wallace. This may, of course, represent a legendary tradition rather than historical fact. The Baillies who held Lamington from 1368 probably built the tower house on Mains farm in the sixteenth century, but it is just possible given its siting close to the river that it has an earlier history.

To explore Lamington start from the former parish church, which sits near the central area of a forty acre Roman marching camp. The Roman road at this point runs through the grounds of Lamington House. The church, set in another circular yard, was dedicated to St. Ninian, perhaps because it was on the pilgrimage route from Edinburgh and Biggar through the hills to the Glenkens and the Machars of Wigtownshire to Whithorn. A St. Ninian's Well is sited in Lamington Glen west of the burn. The church, now disused, is being developed by Biggar Museum Trust as an interpretation centre with a stained glass workshop in the gallery area. The plain but pleasing church, rebuilt in 1721 and heightened in 1828, has a fine Romanesque doorway c. 1130-50 in the north wall. It was used as a secure prison for Jacobites in 1715 and was also visited by Burns, who was not enamoured with either the church or the minister, Thomas Mitchell. Burns summed it all up in one of those vicious little poems he often produced –

'A caulder Kirk and in't but few
A caulder Preacher never spak ...'

Lamington village is a sort of quaint, utterly charming transplant, an English Brigadoon in dour Presbyterian Lanarkshire. The model improved village was created between 1837 and 1890 by Alex Dundas Ross Wishaw Baillie-Cochrane, the 1st Lord Lamington. He was one of the 'Young England' group of generous and idealistic young men round Lord John Manners who did so much to turn the Tories under Disraeli into a caring and reforming party, a party of government. At Lamington Mr. Baillie-Cochrane spent vast sums of money creating an elegant estate, a great house, gardens with waterfalls and rustic bridges, and on building splendidly picturesque and quite excellent houses for his employees and their families and an Episcopalian chapel to cater for their spiritual needs.

From the former parish church take the road past the School, two fine detached cottages and the manse across the bridge over the Lamington Burn. Continue along this road to the Mains to view Lamington Tower from the distance and return to the village. Turn left along the village street by Wayside Cottage, Ashley, Bell View, Tinto View and the Sheiling: cross the A702 to note the marvellous conservation group of houses opposite. Holy Trinity Church (1857) has been taken over by Biggar Museum Trust, perhaps as a centre for Baillie and Lamington family history. The parsonage, now Opportunity House, is on the west side of the A702.

For a walk with views over the Clyde to Tinto and Quothquan Law and over Lamington Glen and into the wild hill country beyond, take the public road south of the church from the A702 up by Hillhouse and Baitlaws to Bleakfield. Note the cultivation terraces on the lower slopes of Lamington Hill (987302) opposite Baitlaws.

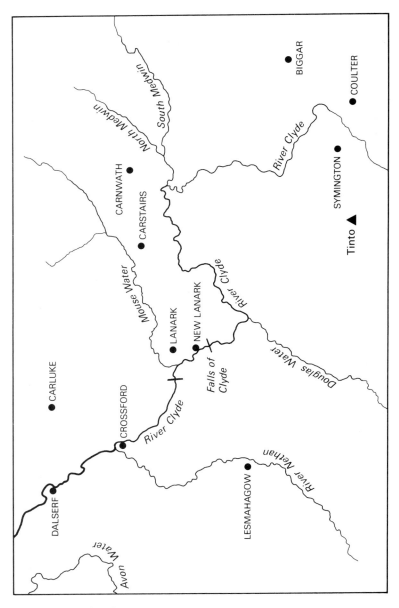

Coulter to Dalserf.

CHAPTER 4

Round Tinto: Coulter, Biggar,
Thankerton and Carnwath

The Clyde goes round Tinto following an almost comically
convoluted course from Coulter by Covington and Carnwath
and Carstairs before turning south-west to the old Carmichael
Boat crossing at Hyndford Bridge. Obviously over 200 or 500 or
1,000 years the river has changed its course many times,
particularly across the flood plain where it is joined by the North
and South Medwin at The Meetings. It is more difficult to assess
changes in other areas, for example, at Crawford and Lamington
or at Castledykes, where the river in the Roman period ran close
to the fort. The Clyde is now on the whole controlled and
contained by embankments and causeways, and the bridges at
Wolfclyde and Thankerton and near Carstairs Junction have
replaced the fords and boats or ferry floats.

A remarkable feature of the area, quite apart from the rich
diversity of scenery from Border glens to fenlike fields, is the
number of parishes, Coulter, Biggar, Covington with (from
1770) Thankerton, Libberton with (from 1660) Quothquan,
Symington, Pettinain, Carnwath, Carstairs and Carmichael, and,
on the periphery, Walston, Dunsyre and Dolphinton. These
probably represent twelfth and thirteenth century landholdings
and the various sub-divisions and amalgamations that took place
at that time.

Coulter

Travelling north on the A702 from Lamington the road drops
down quite suddenly into the wholly delightful and enchanting
world of Coulter (pronounced as 'Kuter'), where only the
eccentricities of spelling are beyond disbelief. It is not the
same Culter or Culthar as the Maryculter on the Dee in
Kincardineshire where Walter Byset founded one of the two
Scottish houses of the Knights Templars *c.*1221-36 (the other
house was in Midlothian). The twelfth or thirteenth century
castle of Alexander de Cutir, the family taking its name from the
place, was above the ford at Wolfclyde, just north of the bridge

carrying the A72. The motte is small and no trace of the bailey and ditches or outer defences are visible. The parish church sits in a beautifully sheltered spot more than a mile away from the castle behind Culter Allers House. It is substantially a building of 1810, but incorporates much earlier work.

Coulter is a world of commuters and country gentlemen. It had its own railway station at Wolfclyde on the Symington, Biggar and Broughton line from 1860 up to 1951. The cluster of country houses in or close to the village is unusual. Cornhill House built to plans by William Leiper for Alexander Kay in 1871, Coulter Mains House built in 1838 for the antiquarian Adam Sim. and Culter Allers House built in 1880 are all essentially in the Scottish Baronial tradition. Culter House in a fine parkland setting with a 'Mile' long ride or avenue (C.1746) running behind it has the simple elegance of an earlier era. The centre portion was built in 1688 for Alexander Menzies and the wings added shortly thereafter. The Menzies family held the estate from 1605 to 1771, when the last land was sold off to the Baillies of Lamington and the Dicksons of Kilbucho and Hartree. Note also the lodges at Cornhill and at Culter House, each in keeping with its own big house behind. The Culter Mains ford is said to have been called Sandys Ford after the 4th laird, Alexander Menzies, 'a person of dissipated habits' who was careless enough to get himself drowned while crossing the Clyde 'when intoxicated': an unlikely explanation of the placename, but a neat story!

Coulter village, a sweet mixture of single storey nineteenth century handloom weavers' cottages and two storey houses, is worth exploring in detail. Note in particular Coulter Square, Coulter Library (1838 and 1888), and the restored early nine-teenth century corn mill which opened in November 1990 as Culter Mill Restaurant. The children in the primary school are encouraged to take an active interest in local history and archaeology and recent projects have included the construction of an Iron Age house and a souterrain.

The hinterland behind the village up the Culter Water is magnificent Border hillwalking country, fortunately not polluted by tax concession trees. The concentration of Iron Age hill forts, especially Cow Castle east of Nisbet, and White Hill and Mitchelhill Rings above the 'hidden' valley with the site of Kilbucho church, is an almost unique group. Note also the cultivation terraces on

Clydesdales at Biggar Show, July 1990. (*Lanark Gazette* photograph).

Culter Crags (028336), like the Lamington group on a hillside facing south-west. Keen walkers should explore the roads up to Culter Waterhead and Cowgill Lower and Upper Reservoirs, remembering the extraordinary history of railway engineering operations in the area, and up to the remains of the bastle at Windgate House. Culter Fell, at 2454 feet the highest point in the area, is the centrepiece of a jigsaw of rolling hills which can be traversed either south-west towards Coomb Dod and Camps Reservoir above Crawford or south-east to Glenwhappen Rig and the Kingledores Burn and to the A701 south of Broughton. The Dumfries-Edinburgh and the Peebles-Broughton-Biggar bus services can be used to get back to a starting point in Coulter or Biggar.

A gentler walk or run by car is from Coulter Church up the hill towards Crosscryne for a wonderful panoramic view over Hartree to Biggar, Quothquan Law and Tinto. From Crosscryne either continue down the steep hill road by Hartree to Biggar or continue east by Howstack and Gosland to Broughton. The Border country here, a world of sheep farms and hill cattle, the world of *Witch Wood* and *John Burnet of Barns*, is very much the home of John Buchan (1875-1940), 1st Lord Tweedsmuir. The old Free Church at the south end of Broughton on the A701 is now the John Buchan Centre with a collection of memorabilia and photographs dealing with the lives of Buchan and his sister Anna ('O. Douglas'). One of the stained glass windows was in memory of a local family called Hannay. Buchan's grandfather, John Masterton, was the tenant of Broughton Green, and his father, the Reverend John Buchan, worked for six months as depute for the Free Church minister in Broughton.

The local writer, Gilbert Rae (1875-1955), who walked the roads between Thankerton and Broughton and Dawyck as an apprentice ironmonger and bagman, provided a vivid picture of life in the area before the Second World War. Look in particular for copies of his collections of short stories and character sketches, for *Sandy McCrae of Hirpleben* (1947), which has some great descriptions of an over genteel Burns Supper and the Christmas Eve concert at the local Curlin' Club, and *In the Howe o' Braefoot* (1951), which has a glorious account of the campaign in the Conservative interest by Colonel Dewsdrop of Doosdale.

Biggar

The road into Biggar from Hartree passes the 10-acre site at Hartreemill purchased in 1979 by Biggar Rugby F.C. (founded only in 1975) and the remains of Boghall Castle. The fourteenth/fifteenth century castle of the Flemings, who became Earls of Wigtoun in 1606, was a large and important fortress with curtain walls and corner towers and water-filled moat. It had a stirring history with sieges in 1568 and 1650. Notable visitors included James V and Mary Queen of Scots. Although restored in 1650 it fell into disrepair in the later eighteenth century and was largely demolished in 1839. A fifteenth century hackbut gun, possibly French, found at the castle in 1873, is now in the Moat Park Museum.

The fields on the Hartree road are sometimes the quarters of those massive, gentle, calm creatures, leggy youngsters and venerable old gentlemen, the Clydesdale horses. The Clydesdales emerged in Lanarkshire as a distinctive breed in the eighteenth century out of a mixture of local packhorse mares and Flemish stallions. Famous stallions and mares from Lochlyoch and Lampits and from other farms round Tinto and Lanark and Carnwath

Covington Tower and Dovecot from the north-east.

helped to build up the breed with its enormous power and capacity for hard work, for example in clearing new farm land in Canada and Australia in the later nineteenth and early twentieth century. Interestingly the greatest Scottish painter of horses was James Howe of Skirling (1780-1836). His paintings of the horse and stallion fairs at Skirling in 1829 are reproduced in A. D. Cameron's *The Man Who Loved to Draw Horses* (1986).

Biggar has only in recent years become a world of museums, but it has had a long history as a strategic junction. The A702 into Biggar follows closely the line of the Roman road from Coulter by the Free Church Wood, Springfield, Causewayend and Biggar Park. It probably continued through the town more or less on the line of the present main street. There must also be a very good chance of there having been a Roman fort or fortlet in the Biggar area to patrol the Gap and the routes north-east to the Forth and north-west along the Clyde to Castledykes.

To discover the town, which became a burgh of barony in 1451, note first Baldwin's castle mound *c.*1150 in the manse garden just below the junction of the B7016 Carnwath road and the A702. The local folk no doubt lived in a cluster of houses round the castle and the church of St. Nicholas, which was on the same site as the cruciform collegiate church to the Blessed Mary of Biggar founded by Malcolm, Lord Fleming in 1545/6. The church, now Biggar Kirk, was to have a provost and eight prebendaries, including a master and a teacher of the School of Song and an instructor in the Grammar School, and four choirboys, and a hospice for six bedesmen. As the last pre-Reformation religious foundation in Scotland it is striking evidence of the continuing vitality of the old Scottish church. The building, with dressed stone from Libberton quarry, was altered in 1870 and restored in 1934-35. Its founder was killed at the battle of Pinkie in 1547.

The complex of museums under the Biggar Museum Trust is quite extraordinary for such a small town. The earliest, Gladstone Court Museum, opened in May 1968. It contains a series of folk museum type reconstructions of local life in Victorian and Edwardian times, the telephone exchange, the photographer's studio, the schoolroom, and the wee shops, an ironmonger, a bootmaker, a dressmaker, a chemist, a jeweller, a printer. The Moat Park Heritage Centre opened in June 1988 in the former North United Presbyterian Church of 1865 – 66 is a lively local history museum for the Upper Ward area. The comprehensive local Archives also contain the records of the Albion Motor Car Company founded in 1899. These include the job sheets on microfilm for 164,000 vehicles from 1900 to 1961. Biggar is also the centre of the annual August Blackwood Murray Run with 200 lorries and cars and tractors. The Trust's vehicle collection includes a magnificent early Albion Dog Cart Car.

Greenhill, now a Covenanters' Museum, was transplanted and rebuilt between 1975 and 1981 from its original site in Wiston parish to the Burn Braes below Biggar Kirk. It is a mid seventeenth century and early eighteenth century laird's farmhouse.

The Trust has also acquired the former parish churches at Walston and Lamington and Holy Trinity at Lamington, and Brownsbank farm cottage near Candy Mill where Hugh McDiarmid (1892-1978) lived and worked for twenty-seven years from 1951. His widow, Valda, continued to live there until her death in 1989. Brownsbank is to become a centre for writers in residence.

There is also at the bottom of the town the Biggar Gas Works (1839-73) Museum, an outstation of the Royal Museum of

The Wee Bush Inn, Carnwath (1750) - 'Better a Wee Bush than nae Bield'.

Scotland. It is a remarkable example of a virtually complete small gas-making plant built in 1839 to supply the town with gas lighting. It was rebuilt and expanded in 1914. The two gas holders of 1858 and 1879 were rebuilt in 1918 and 1939. The smells are included gratis.

At the other end of the town on the Broughton Road is the Biggar Little Theatre which was opened in 1986. It is the headquarters of the famous Purves Puppets and is a centre for exhibitions and workshops and the performance of puppet plays.

In the town centre the Corn Exchange built in 1860-61 to plans by David McGibbon is used for stage performances by Biggar Theatre Workshop. Note in front of it the circular 'concrete poem' by Ian Hamilton Finlay of Stonypath near Dunsyre. It was unveiled in 1970 by Lady Tweedsmuir.

Note on both sides of the High Street from the seventeenth century pack horse style Cadger's, or pedlar's, Brig the number of period eighteenth and nineteenth century houses and inns with lintel dates from 1755, 1744, 1671, 1697, 1698, and the narrow pends and closes to the 'crofts' behind. The wide main road for markets and fairs and the narrow strips of land behind show how much the town has retained its late mediaeval layout. Other traditions, the Biggar Play and the Burning Out of the Old Year in a huge Hogmanay fire in the High Street, are also still very much part of the present.

Thankerton and Symington

For Thankerton take the Lindsaylands Road at the Cadger's Brig in Biggar, passing the motte at Wolfclyde on the south, and continue along the Clyde by Cormiston and Cormiston Towers, looking south across the river to the sand and gravel-pitted landscape on the other bank. Quothquan Law on the north is an Iron Age hill fort. Cross the Clyde by the hump-backed Thankerton Bridge which replaced the Boat Ferry in 1778. This is a good short walk from Biggar connecting with the Lanark to Biggar bus service in Thankerton.

Thankerton and Symington both expanded in the later nineteenth century as holiday and commuter villages with visitors and residents using the Tinto Express to Glasgow. They each took their name from twelfth century Norman Flemish settlers, Tancard and Symon Loccard. Thankerton parish was joined to Covington in 1770. The site of its ancient St. John's Kirk, the Church of the Wudechirche or the Church of Tanchardstone, is in the rounded churchyard enclosure near the Kirk Burn between the A72 and the A73 north-west of Symington.

The A73 between Carmichael and Symington via Fallburn Toll was constructed across the moorland about 1800 using rafts of brushwood as a foundation. It replaced the old road south by Howgate Mouth. Tinto Hill (2320 feet) is a steady uphill ramble from the carpark at Fallburn along a track across heather moorland and over red felsite scree. En route note the 60 yard diameter fort above Fallburn (961367) with remarkably deep ditches and double concentric ramparts. The Karyn de Tintou is a fine Bronze Age cairn some 18 feet high and 45 yards in diameter. Adding a stone may not make your wishes come true, but it is better than throwing one at the hang gliders who sometimes use the hill. The views across the Clyde and to the Pentland Hills to the north and north-east, to the blue hills of Tweeddale to the south-east and possibly to Goatfell in Arran to the west are magnificent. The popular mocking verse included

Carstairs village green, laid out by Mr Henry Monteith in 1826.

in Robert Chambers' *The Popular Rhythms of Scotland* (1826) is perhaps a comment on human pride and fallibility.

> On Tintock-tap there is a mist,
> And in that mist there is a kist,
> And in that kist there is a caup,
> And in that caup there is a drap;
> Tak up the caup, drink aff the drap,
> And set the caup on Tintock-tap.

Underneath Scaut Hill and above Tintoside farm is the remains of Fatlips Castle, a tower house in a position as striking as it is secretive. Symington village has had a second wave of growth and expansion in the last twenty years. The church, rebuilt in 1761 and enlarged in 1821, is on the south-east side of the village. The churchyard has a watch-tower built as a precaution against the snatching of bodies for the use of medical students in Edinburgh and Glasgow. Symington House, completed in 1915 by Andrew Prentice, was one of the last Scottish country houses.

Covington, Pettinain, Quothquan, Libberton

The most striking feature of this stretch of the Clyde is the extent to which, even in the nineteenth century, the river was a barrier between Covington and Pettinain on one side and Quothquan and Libberton on the other. Of course there were fords, between Covington and Quothquan, betweeen Pettinain and Carnwath (the Black Pot), between Pettinain and Carstairs (the Langfurde and Mary's Ford), and the famous Lampits ferry float; but there was no bridge until the Eastfield to Carstairs Junction road bridge was opened in 1914.

Travelling north from Thankerton to the west of the Clyde note first the row of six early nineteenth century single storey cottages almost opposite the school at Newtown of Covington. Surprisingly they are numbered as 82 to 92 East Side. This is an outstanding group of Lowland housing with thatched roofing underneath the present corrugated iron.

The classic grouping of castle and church at Covington is also quite outstanding. The tower house, probably c.1420-40, was built by the Lindsays who held Covington from c.1368 to 1679. It is set within an extensive complex of the rectangular defences of an earlier mediaeval moated manor. The area round the tower is about 150 feet square and the outer ditches enclose an area of about 450 feet by 350 feet. These may be the remains of the later twelfth century 'villa Colbani'. Colban and his son Merevin were Norman Flemish settlers. The fifteenth or sixteenth century circular dovecot close to the road has 500 boxes.

The church on a twelfth century site includes three very fine deeply splayed fifteenth century Gothic traceried windows which lit the altar, the rood screen and the nave. The church was restored in 1903. Note also to the south the quite utterly charming former manse of Covington.

It can only enhance the ambience of the whole to mention that Robert Burns stayed at Covington Mains en route from Edinburgh to Ayrshire.

One of the best ways to explore the area is to take the early evening (6 p.m.) Lanark to Leadhills service bus. Its route is via Pettinain, Swaites, Covington and Thankerton, so there are excellent views north to the watery world of the Clyde beyond Southholm and Townhead and south-east to Quothquan Law, which looks a much more exciting and dominating hill from this side. Note also the road south-west to Cairngryffe Hill (1000 feet) quarry.

Pettinain (Pedynnane) church on its raised hill looks from

the south like some miniature Lanarkshire Ely. The handsome little church dates from c.1696, with alterations in 1820 and internal work in 1870. The site dates from c.1140 or earlier. Syrand the priest was resident here c.1147. The large former manse looks more appropriate for some Victorian Norfolk rural dean with a very large family than for a Presbyterian minister in one of the smallest parishes in Scotland. Note also the village row of cottages north-west of the church. In 1794 the village population was 110 with another 276 people in the country part of the parish. There were also 90 working and 44 young horses.

East of the Clyde Quothquan, which includes Biggar Common and Quothquan Law, was combined with Libberton parish in 1660. The church was ruinous by the later eighteenth century. The rounded churchyard includes the burial aisle of the Chancellors of Shieldhill. Shieldhill, a hotel since 1959, is now a rather elegant establishment catering for an international clientele. It incorporates parts of the fifteenth or sixteenth century tower house with additions in 1820 and later. A new and welcome resident in the parish in 1990 is the former British and American Open golf champion Mr. Tony Jacklin.

The B7016 hill road from Biggar by Carwood and Whitecastle has fine views across over Libberton parish and to Carstairs and Carnwath. Libberton church (1812) is on a twelfth century or earlier site. The manse is now a private house. The old village near the church has virtually disappeared, but new houses have been completed in 1990. John Fraser, writing in the Statistical Account in 1791, mentions the existence of three large penned vaults (? souterrains) in the village as asylums for cattle.

Carnwath and Carstairs

After the Medwin Water on the B7016 to Carnwath note the dismantled railway line before Bankhead. This was the Caledonian Railway branch line from Carstairs Junction by Dunsyre to Dolphinton, which carried passenger services from 1867 to 1945. Dolphinton, with a population of about 25, had two railway stations. The Leadburn, Linton and Dolphinton Railway, taken over by North British in 1866, provided a link east to the Peebles to Edinburgh line at Leadburn Junction from 1864 to 1933.

The great motte on the golf course west of Carnwath was built by William de Somerville c.1140. The de Somervilles from

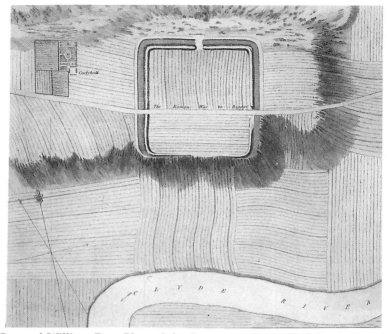

General William Roy, Plan of the Roman station called Castle-dykes near Carstairs (drawn in 1753), from *The Military Antiquities of the Romans in Scotland* (1793). Note Corbyhall and 'The Roman Way to Biggar'.

Yorkshire held Libberton including Carnwath and Linton in Tweeddale. The motte – view from the A70 – has exceptionally steep sides and a small area on top. Modern landscaping has obliterated the deep ditch and large bailey mound still visible in 1794. The entrance may have been through a tunnel at the base of the motte and then up through a sort of stairway inside the mound into a wooden blockhouse on the top.

From the later thirteenth century to 1602 the Somerville's main strength was Couthally or Quodaily Castle between the B7016 and the railway line north of Carnwath. The site was a sort of promontory with water defences jutting out into the swampland on three sides. Further north on the B7016 note at Eastshield, north of the Dippool Water, the remains of the Inglis' sixteenth century tower house with dovecot on top.

Carmichael Estate with the House and the former gardens - aerial photograph taken in 1981.

The parish church near the motte became the site of a collegiate foundation for a provost and six prebendaries and eight bedesmen established by Thomas de Somerville in 1424. The Gothic north transept, St. Mary's Aisle, is now the mausoleum of the Lockharts of Lee and Carnwath. It contains fifteenth century effigies of Lord and Lady Somerville. The modern church was designed by David Bryce in 1867.

The village became a burgh of barony in 1451. Note the seventeenth century market cross. The tradition of the (Red) Hose Race on the Feast of St. John the Baptist dating back to 1508 is still maintained, although it is now held in the Memorial Park in August instead of June. The footrace for a pair of hose, half an ell of English cloth, was originally from the east end of the town to the Cawlo Cross. *The Red Hose* (1879), a novel by William Scott, who was born in Carnwath in 1832 and became editor of the *Birmingham Daily Globe,* is about a series of accidental deaths amongst members of the Biggar Club of Ancient Doubters. It is set in the Biggar/Carnwath area in the reign of George IV. A copy may be consulted in the Mitchell Library in Glasgow.

The long main street in Carnwath includes some very good

and unspoiled nineteenth century houses and inns. The thatched Wee Bush Inn, built in 1750 on the road from Ayr to Edinburgh, was and still is a popular establishment. Robert Burns stayed here in 1786 and may, or may not, have scratched the motto from his own coat of arms on a windowpane – 'Better a Wee Bush than nae Bield'. There is no question about his interest in heraldry, which was quite genuine.

North of Carnwath the £75 million golf and leisure complex at a 477 acre site at Kersewell Mains is to include an indoor equestrian centre, a curling centre, a clay pigeon shooting range and a championship golf course with Tony Jacklin as designer consultant. The plans for the hotel in the form of a massive rounded Iron Age house are exciting. Planning permission was approved by Clydesdale District Council in March 1991. The impact on the area could be both beneficial and profound.

Dominating the landscape south-west of Carnwath on 200 acres of what had been Lampits farmland in Carstairs Hospital. Since it was under the 'Criminal Lunatics Department' of the prison service in 1939 it has had several changes of name from the 'Emergency Medical Service Hospital for Neurosis', the 'Ministry Hospital for Psychotics', and the 'State Institution for Mental Defectives' in 1948 to the State (Mental) Hospital.

The major post 1847 railway depot at Carstairs Junction is now with electrification and modernisation programmes in the British Rail network increasingly less important in national and local terms. Carstairs Junction is a distinct and different village from Carstairs a mile away to the north-west.

Carstairs House, built in 1824 to plans by William Burn for Henry Monteith, who purchased the estate in 1819, is an enormous and pretentious Tudor-Gothic mansion house. The grounds include a mausoleum in the form of a classical temple and a circular domed ice house. The private electric railway built in the 1880s by Joseph Monteith from the house to his lodge gates at the Junction 1½ miles away must have been an extraordinary foible. It was powered from dynamo driven water turbines at Cleghorn mill on the Mouse Water via a 4 mile long overhead cable. The house was purchased by the Diocese of Glasgow in 1911 and became St. Charles Hospital for children. Since 1987 as Monteith House it has been a private nursing home.

Carstairs village has an interesting history. The stone castle of

The Third International Carmichael Clan Gathering, Carmichael House, 30 June 1990. Richard Carmichael of Carmichael addressing the gathering. (*Lanark Gazette* photograph).

the Bishops of Glasgow at Casteltarras was built by Bishop Robert Wishart *c.*1292. In 1522 the castle was 'rentellet' to Sir James Hamilton of Finnart. It was located near the parish church which was substantially rebuilt in 1794 on the site of the mediaeval St. Mary's. The village became a burgh of barony in 1765 without any obvious benefit as it was still a muddle of dunghills and peat stacks in the 1790s. The new model planned village with the open green was laid out by Mr. Monteith c.1826, and it has retained this layout to the present day.

South-west of Carstairs off the A70 at Corbiehall is Castledykes Roman fort. Some traces of the multiple ditches and the six yard thick rampart can still be located. The fort and the road or 'causeway' were, of course, much more clearly defined when William Roy prepared his plan there in 1753. The Roman temporary camps at Spittal near Carstairs and at two sites (928446 and 924447) near Corbiehall, and the roads from Tweeddale on a line west of Bankhead and south of Lampits and from Coulter or Biggar along the Clyde to Castledykes are not visible above the ground.

Carmichael and Hyndford

From Castledykes the Clyde ripples south passing a series of old corn mills at Millhill and Carmichael on to the site of the Carmichael Boat and ford, which became redundant in 1773 when Hyndford Bridge designed by Alexander Stevens was completed. Note also the early nineteenth century toll house.

Carmichael estate to the east has belonged to the Carmichaels for probably at least 700 years. Richard of Karemigel and Gamel of Hindeford in 1259 took their names from the places in which they lived. The original church of Kirkmychel was probably on the Kirkhill south-east of East Mains. There was a St. Michael's Well below to the south. The Kirkhill itself is very precipitous and may have been a hill fort before it was taken over by the church. Note also the larger hill fort on Chester Hill on the north side of the A73.

John Carmichael, the 3rd Earl of Hyndford, who was a British envoy in Prussia and Russia in the 1740s, was probably the key figure in the development of the estate in the eighteenth century from the building of Carmichael House in 1734 on the site of the fourteenth century castle to laying out the formal avenues and gardens and the lesser estate buildings, including the circular dovecot at West Mains. The ruins of Carmichael House with the fine pavilions and gable ends still suggest something of the elegance of the original.

A fine solid new church with a laird's loft and an outside stair brought from Kirkhill was built in 1750 at the crossroads beyond

Westgate. Note the two windows in the south wall by Sir Robert Lorimer completed in 1905.

The present laird, Richard Carmichael of Carmichael, has combined managing the estate as a whole, including a deer farm, a saw mill and the direct marketing of venison, beef, lamb and timber, with a positive and innovative programme of securing the interest and support of Carmichaels overseas in the future of the Clan Carmichael. A popular and highly successful Third International Clan Carmichael Gathering was held in July 1990 with Carmichaels from the New World and Kaermiggelts from Holland. In the long term it may be possible to establish a clan heritage and estate interpretation centre in the woodland near Carmichael House. The eagles and pineapples on the Eagle Gate on the A73 were brought there from Westraw in Pettinain.

CHAPTER 5

The Falls of Clyde, Lanark and New Lanark

Until Hyndford Bridge was opened in 1773 there were five fords and ferries between the Carmichael Boat and the Falls of Clyde. The last, the Tillieford, upstream from Bonnington Linn, was important for traffic between Douglas and the town of Lanark. West of the Falls the main ferry crossing until the Clydesholm Bridge was built between 1695 and 1699 was just upstream from the site of the bridge and hence up St. Patrick's Road to Castlebank.

The stretch of the Clyde between Hyndford Bridge and the meeting with the Douglas Water below Crookboat is very interesting. Either drive by car or take a Glespin, Douglas or Muirkirk bus along the A70, passing Howford and the Carmichael road on the left, to the first road (at 904400) on the right. Note the old Carstairs, Lanark and Muirkirk Railway line coming in from the north and the site of the railway bridge over the river west of Prett's Mill. Walk along the road which goes delightfully through the farm at Prett's Mill and then twists up and down beside the old railway line with good views to Tinto, the Douglas Water and Harperfield. The view from Crookboat farm as the Clyde goes into an extraordinary U bend is a tremendous surprise, in fact quite breathtaking in its directness and simplicity. Further on the long walk or car run by the Douglasmouth Bridge north of Sandilands and hence north by Gowkknowe, Damhill and Corehouse Farm is an unusual approach to the West Lodge (877414) for access to the Falls of Clyde Scottish Wildlife Trust Reserve.

Approaching Lanark from the east by the A73 note on the right the Winston Barracks on a 44 acre site developed by the War Office between 1936 and 1939 and on the left the Hyndford Sand and Gravel Quarry works. The vast Lanark Moor Country Park on common ground held as the property of the community includes the Lanark Golf Club, founded 1851, which is a regional qualifying course for the Open, and Lanark Loch, which was developed from swamp land between 1832 and 1840 as a water supply for the town. Lanark Race Course has a long history of horse racing dating back to the first thirty years of the seventeenth century and a fairly continuous record of races between the eighteenth century and 1977. The famous Silver Bell trophy was made in Edinburgh by a goldsmith called Lindsay between 1608 and 1610. The Race Course also has an interesting place in British aviation history before the Great War as the site of Ewing's School of Flying. Note on the south side of the A73 the rough road, The Beeches, for access by walkers to New Lanark.

The late nineteenth century Auction Market in a 12½ acre site (post 1867) on Hyndford Road is probably the most important building in Lanark in terms of trade and commerce. It is also a place all visitors should find their way to, especially for the busy Monday vegetable, plant and dairy produce market. Lanark is a meeting place for local folk from all points of the compass and it is an interesting exercise just to listen to the different voices and dialect intonations and to try to work out whether someone is from Crawford or Biggar or Lesmahagow or The Forth. The best textbook is the *Linmill Stories* (Edinburgh 1990) by Robert McLellan (1907-85). The stories, written in the early 1960s but set in the earlier part of the century, are written in the dialect with which he was familiar from staying with his grandparents at Linmill farm between Kirkfieldbank and Hazelbank.

In Ladyacre Road visit the Clyde Valley Tourist Board head-quarters in the Horsemarket for brochures, advice and details of the local bus timetables. The bus station has an amazingly diverse selection of services to Biggar, Leadhills, Hamilton, Glasgow, Glespin, Douglas, Muirkirk, Lesmahagaow, Carnwath, Carstairs, New Lanark and Forth, operated by several different companies. The chaos is often total - it helps if you recognise the bus driver! The railway station offers a service on the branch line opened in 1855 to Glasgow via Carluke, Wishaw and Motherwell. Note the cluster of railway period hotels in Bannatyne St. and, from the train going out of Lanark, the castellated Smyllum House built in 1790 for Sir William Honeyman. *Scotland on Sunday* ran an excellent report (23/12/90) on the shoddy story of the decline in the fortunes of this house since 1985.

The prominent church spire on the south side of Bannatyne St. belongs to St. Mary's Church, completed in 1910 for the Order of St. Vincent de Paul to replace the older (1857-1907) church.

This part of Lanark east of the High St. is very much the modern burgh, although the site of the mediaeval Hospital of St. Leonard (pre 1249) was in the St. Leonard Street area, and St. Kentigern's Church, the mediaeval parish church of Lanark, is in the large graveyard opposite the Auction Market. The surviving north aisle with pointed arches and pillars is probably fifteenth century, but this was the site of the church which David I assigned to the Premonstratensian canons of Dryburgh Abbey *c.*1150. They also maintained a chapel dedicated to St. Nicholas *in* the town of Lanark at the bottom of the later High Street on the site of the eighteenth century parish church. The puzzle is why the twelfth century church was located so far away from the castle and the town. Was the hilltop site with its dedication to St. Kentigern already a much older Christian place of worship? The graveyard includes a memorial vault (1931) to William Smellie (1697-1763), the 'Master of British Midwifery'. Smellie, the traveller William Lithgow (1582-1650), the painter Gavin Hamilton (1723-98), the judge Lord Braxfield (1722-99), the General William Roy were Lanark Grammar School's most famous pupils.

It is difficult to get used to the rather perverse Lanark logic that the castle and the mediaeval town are at the bottom of the 'Hie Toun' or later High Street which had the open Puddin' Burn running down it until 1834. In turn the great and royal castle, the motte of *c.*1140-50, was at the foot of the Castlegate and Broomgate looming over the Delves or Gulleytudlem hollow below. The old town was set around and between the Bloomgate, Broomgate, Castlegate and Wellgate and the North Vennel.

Lanark probably became a burgh in the 1140s. 1140 is only an intelligent guess and is at least as good as 1139 or 1149, but there is no direct evidence to prove the point. As the administrative centre of the sheriffdom by 1159 or earlier it was a place of some importance. The oldest surviving Scottish burgh charter, for Ayr, was signed here *c.*1203-06 under William the Lion (1165-1214): Alexander III may have had a mint in Lanark during the earlier part of his reign (1249-86): and the Scottish Parliament met here in 1293, 94 and 95. A Franciscan Priory in the Bloomgate, Friar's Lane, Broomgate area was founded by Robert I. *c.*1325-26.

Robert I took the castle and town in 1310, but it is the part played by William Wallace in the rebellion in 1297-98 against

Edward I with the aim of restoring John Balliol to the throne of Scotland that became an integral part of local folklore. Much of Blind Harry's tale of the Wallace written in the 1470s in the reign of James III belongs to the Douglas Fairbanks senior/Errol Flynn/Kevin Costner 'Robin Hood School of History'. In other words it is impossible to disentangle hard fact from romantic fiction and cherished legend. The statue of Wallace by the self-taught sculptor Robert Forrest given to the town in 1822 and placed on the front of St. Nicholas Church facing the High Street is in terms of appearance, physique and dress part of the legend.

Wallace's family had extensive landholdings in Scotland from the Paisley and Elderslie area in Renfrewshire to as far north as the Moray Firth and it seems likely that William, as a younger son, learned his skills in the art of war and developed his leadership qualities with Edward I's armies in Wales and France. Blind Harry's account of the reasons for Wallace killing Sir William Heselrig, the English sheriff at Lanark, in May 1297 is wholly unreliable – it is not possible to know whether this was a matter of personal vengeance because of Heselrig's responsibility for the death of Wallace's wife or mistress, Marion Braidfute, or whether it was a political statement against an alien ruler and a calculated act of defiance and rebellion against Edward I. In a short and brilliant career Wallace defeated the English at Stirling in 1297, was Guardian of Scotland between March and December 1298, was defeated at Falkirk in July 1298, fled to France, and returned to Scotland to conduct a guerilla campaign between 1303 and 1305 in Annandale, Liddesdale and Cumberland. He was captured near Glasgow on 3 August and executed in London on 22 August, 1305. The charges of treason, murder, arson and sacrilege referred specifically only to the murder of Heselrig at Lanark.

Whuppity Scoorie and Lanimers

Lanark has maintained two fine old traditions. Whuppity Scoorie, which takes place at 6p.m. on the 1st of March, is essentially an exorcism ceremony. The church bells are rung to warn demons away and then young children run three times round St. Nicholas Church beating each other with paper balls on the ends of two feet long strings, i.e. beating out the evil spirits and chasing away Winter and welcoming in the Spring.

The spirit of Lanimers, Lanark, June 1990. *(Lanark Gazette* photograph).

The Lanimers from 6th to 12th June is the centre of the year for many 'Lanarkians' and their families. I have seen it suggested that the male of the species is permitted to forget his dog's inoculation or his wedding anniversary, but not to miss Lanimer Day. Since the post Reformation period in the 1570s Lanimers has been essentially based on the Riding of the Marches, inspecting the old burgh boundary marker stones, for example on the Mouse Water below Lockhart Mill and above the Leechford, with associated festivities and street processions. In the mediaeval burgh the June ceremonies were associated essentially with the festival of Corpus Christi inaugurated by Urban IV in 1262, that is with the yearly performance of morality plays and religious processions. The burgh records from 1488 on to the 1550s show the council allocating payments for these processions, for mending the Cross, for items for Christ to wear, for the dragon and St. George. It is also possible and indeed likely that the tradition goes back much further into the fourteenth or even the thirteenth century, and that it may have included a specific interest in recording and confirming burgh precincts.

Walks round Lanark

To explore the old town start from St. Nicholas Church and walk down the Castlegate by the site of the Port and The Butts to the great mount of Lanark Castle. The upper level of the motte was excavated and levelled in the eighteenth century to become a bowling green, now the premises of the Lanark Thistle Bowling Club; even with the great ditch on the north filled in it is still an impressive sight, best appreciated from the air. St. Patrick's Road to the west led down to the Clydesholm ferry: some of the income from the ferry was used in the 1550s for the upkeep of the town's archery butts.

Return to the High St. by the Broomgate. The eighteenth and early nineteenth century houses along the Broomgate, the Castlegate and the Wellgate are probably on the same sites as the earlier mediaevel wooden houses. Recent excavations by the Lanark and District Archaeological Society have yielded evidence of thirteenth and fourteenth century pottery and iron slag and copper workings in the Broomgate, Bloomgate and Castlegate areas. The closes (Wide Close, Shirley's Close, Duncan's Close) and the wynds and vennels provide more clues to the mediaeval to seventeenth century street pattern before the eighteenth century realignment of the High Street. Some of the houses with crow-stepped gables are seventeenth century: note, for example, the IH 1688 IM marriage stone in 10-16 High Street.

The spacious Georgian St. Nicholas Church, 'the Laigh Kirk', completed in 1774 and the Tolbooth (2-8 High St.), built in 1778-79 on the site of the fifteenth century tolbooth, and the Clydesdale Hotel (1793) in the Bloomgate where the Wordsworths and Coleridge lodged in 1803 provide a contrast in eighteenth century refined elegance. Maisie's Bar (12-14 Wellgate) makes an interesting contrast to the Clydesdale Hotel.

Turn into Hope Street and continue as far as the Scottish Episcopal Christ Church, noting the impressive Georgian and Victorian public buildings, the former Council Building (1834) and the Sheriff Court House (1860s), St. Kentigern's Church of Scotland, and the Lindsay Institute (the District Library head-quarters). Lanark, of course, remained a market town and administrative centre in the nineteenth century, but it also benefited from the numerous visitors to the Falls of Clyde and from the bustling proximity of New Lanark.

Lanark Castle - a huge twelfth century motte and thirteenth century castle site, and now Lanark Thistle Bowling Club premises.

Lanark is fairly unique in Lowland Scotland in having so many spectacular landscapes and gorge scenery at the edge of the town. A good short walk is to go up Hope St., turn left into and continue to the end of Waterloo Road and hence down the very steep ancient Stey Brae to Lockhart Mill bridge (877450). Return to Lanark by Mousebank Road. The mansion house just visible above the trees to the south-west is Cartland Bridge Hotel, formerly Baronald. By car take the Mousebank Road from the A73 in Lanark after the Westport to Lockhart Mill bridge and continue uphill by Castlehill farm to run parallel with the Carlisle-Glasgow railway line, returning by the Moor Road to Cartland village and Cartland Mains to the A73.

An expedition to discover the Valley Wood and Cleghorn Glen National Nature Reserves via Leechford is a much more exacting and exciting walk. Go up Hope St. and Cleghorn Road and turn left down Bellefield Road passing Bellefield House (1885) Hospital and the Geest Caledonian Produce fruit and vegetable packing centre. The road turns left at the glasshouses to Jerviswood, the outstanding L plan seventeenth century laird's house of the Livingstones and the Baillies, associated particularly with the Covenanter Robert Baillie. The footpath/bridle track opposite the north entrance to the Geest Caledonian plant goes down to the Valley Wood Reserve. Turn right for the footbridge over the Mouse Water beside the old Leechford. Cross the footbridge (888455) and turn left for a relatively straightforward short walk above the Mouse Water as far as the Fulwood Burn. Return to the footbridge at the Leechford.

The second part of this walk is much tougher and in places really quite dangerous. Continue along the north bank of the Mouse: after about 400 yards the path disappears (it has in fact disintegrated ahead) and it is necessary to go right up to the top of the bank (894456) and continue close to the fields and through woodland until the last 300/400 yard section before Cleghorn Bridge: here a very narrow path runs along the edge of an 80'/100' vertical drop to the water and waterfall below. It is not suitable for children or young dogs. Note the remains of the old Jerviswood Mill tucked in on the south bank of the Mouse below Cleghorn Bridge. The views are truly spectacular and the whole exercise is enormously worthwhile.

The Roman road from Castledykes crossed the Mouse just above Cleghorn Mill and then continued to the west of the marching camp at Cleghorn (910459) north to Collielaw Wood and Kilncadzow. From Cleghorn Mill and Bridge take the Forth bus service back to Lanark.

The Falls of Clyde

In the last two decades of the eighteenth century and for at least the first half of the nineteenth century the Falls of Clyde and the island of Staffa competed for the distinction of being the most sought out attractions in Scotland for travellers and antiquarians in search of 'picturesque beauty'. The Falls were a perfect match to the concept of picturesque beauty which had evolved in

Paul Sandby, View of Cory-Lin on the River Clyde near Lanark, c.1753, in a print published in London in 1778. Note Corra Castle above the falls.

England and Scotland in the 1770s and 1780s and were fixed by William Gilpin (1724-1806) in a series of books on aesthetic theory and the appreciation of landscapes. They represented an ideal combination of a colossal outpouring of the sublime, stunning, stupendous forces of nature, that is satisfying the new Romantic emphasis on intensity of emotions, with the adornments of picturesque pavilions and ruined antiquities. Thomas Pennant (1726-98) was probably the first to draw the attention of the British public to the Falls in his *Tour of Scotland* (1771) and *Tour of Scotland, and Voyage to the Hebrides* (1774-75).

The flights of imagination and the highly stylised language used by Capt. Newte on his visit in 1785 to the Falls, "the first scene of this kind in Great Britain", is typical of the presentation of their "sublime horrors" - "this great body of water, rushing with horrid fury, seems to threaten destruction to the solid rocks that seem to enrage it by their resistance. It boils up from the caverns which itself has formed, as if it were vomited out of the infernal regions. The horrid and incessant din with which this is accompanied unnerves and overcomes the heart."

The most famous artists of the period left their record of the

Falls in a series of paintings and prints. Amongst the earliest are the precise, exact, detailed sketches by Paul Sandby (1730-1809) in the 1750s, published in 1778. These include views of Corra Linn and Corra Castle from above and below the Falls. The finest romantic vision of human frailty dwarfed by the cataracts of Corra Linn is by Jacob More (1740-97). The excellent Alexander Nasmyth (1758-1840) painted the falls at Corra, Bonnington and Stonebyres: the last is a specially successful and dramatic composition. His print of Bonnington Linn was published in James Hall's *Travels in Scotland* (1807). Indeed almost everyone who mattered, J.W.M. Turner, William and Dorothy Wordsworth, found their way to the Falls.

Visitors to the Falls today should explore the area in the first instance from New Lanark. Ideally, time permitting, walk down from Lanark and take the service bus back up the hill. A large car park is situated just above the village within approximately five minutes' walking distance. Parking in the historic village itself is not recommended, especially during the busy summer months. On a second visit for a more leisurely study of the Falls of Clyde Wildlife Reserve drive or walk from Kirkfieldbank via Gilchrist's Nurseries and Byreton, with wonderful views across to New Lanark and Lanark en route, the West Lodge (877414) at Corehouse where there is limited parking available.

From New Lanark continue up river by the Scottish Wildlife Trust Centre in the old dyeworks and the 8' fall at Dundaff Linn (880422). A well-maintained path goes along the quiet riverbank to Bonnington Power Station and then climbs steeply to viewpoints across to Corra Linn (882413). The river goes over the falls here in three leaps, about 90' in all. Continue to cross the river at the weir above Bonnington Linn (883405), where the river boils and pours down some 30'. On the south bank walk down the dirt road and the pathway between Corehouse and Corra Castle. Agile and sure-footed visitors may choose to clamber down the old ways to the river level below the castle, but I could not possibly recommend this. Return to New Lanark by the same route, or better still get your chaffeur to collect you at the West Lodge.

The crumbling greywacke crags and cliffs in the gorge, which the river has cut through so spectacularly, are dangerous. The river below is now held on a much harder outcrop of Old Red Sandstone.

Corra Castle, a fifteenth century Bannatyne tower house, is on a promontory site cut off by a 15' to 20' wide rock-cut ditch and with an amazing 100' vertical drop to the river below. The site is very dangerous. On the north bank of the river above Corra Linn note the remains of Sir James Carmichael of Bonnington's summer house (1708). Corehouse, a fine Tudor-Jacobean house (view from the path near Corra Castle) was built for Lord Corehouse by Edward Blore between 1824 and 1827. Blore was also the architect responsible for Sir Walter Scott's Abbotsford. Sir Walter Scott and then Landseer planned the layout of the grounds and estate policies.

Bonnington (1926-27) and Stonebyres (1927) Stations, designed by Sir Edward MacColl for the Lanarkshire Hydro-Electrics Power Company, fundamentally altered the flow of water through the gorges. The river is now more impressive in the winter months and on the occasional open days when Bonnington Power Station is closed.

The Reserve itself repays detailed study. Note the old primary woodland areas at the edge of the gorge, and especially the oaks and ashes and wych elms; the extraordinary range of mosses and ferns, and the number of small and rare plants in cracks and crevices above the water: the Douglas Firs on the Corehouse side and the carefully managed broad-leaved woodland. The woods in spring and early summer have virtual carpets of bluebells and celandines and anemones and violets. The roe deer and badgers and foxes and red squirrels are altogether more secretive creatures. The rich woodland and riverbank bird life includes some 100 species, everything from spotted flycatchers and treepipits to green sandpipers, sand martins, magpies, dippers, grey herons, kingfishers, sparrowhawks, kestrels, buzzards and even peregrines. Winter visitors may include whooper swans, greylag geese, goosanders and cormorants.

New Lanark

New Lanark in 1990 attracted 120,000 visitors. As a major World Heritage site it is going to have a great many more in the near future. The Victorian and Steam Fairs and the opening in 1990 in Mill 3 (1826) of the Annie McLeod Experience have been a great success. In the last, in which all the latest gadgets and theatrical tricks, lasers and the holograms are used, the ghost of a ten-year old mill girl *c.*1820 takes visitors on a monorail journey

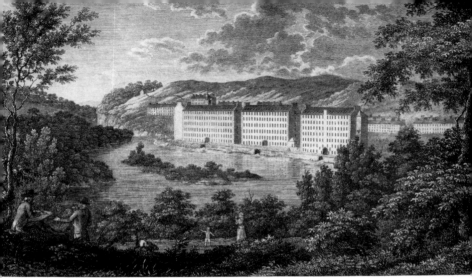

Robert Scott, Lanark Cotton Mills the Property of Robert Owen Esq. and Co.. Scott visited New Lanark in 1799.

through her life experiences and work. Other planned developments include an hotel in Mill 1 and possibly a youth hostel.

It is easy to forget that this interest in David Dale's and Robert Owen's model industrial village was nothing new. Visitors came from all over Europe, Russia, America in the first half of the nineteenth century to inspect and admire the large mills, the profitable and innovative mass production techniques, and the success of first Dale and then Owen in organising men, women and children, many of them from Skye, Argyllshire, Inverness-shire and Caithness, into an efficient, sober and docile work force. The workers, about 1519 under Dale, 2210 under Owen, all lived in New Lanark.

A substantial portfolio of sketches, watercolours and aquatint prints are available for this period, notably by Robert Scott in 1799, John Winning c.1818, and John Clark c.1820. Note in Clark's print, for example, the absence of Mill 3 which was destroyed by fire in 1819 and not replaced until 1826.

New Lanark was conceived, planned and built by David Dale (1739-1806), the Glasgow banker and cloth merchant, first in partnership with Richard Arkwright from 1784 to 1786 and then on his own until he sold out to his son-in-law, Robert Owen, in 1799. Dale ran New Lanark with the same mixture of sound business sense and autocratic paternalism which Owen was to develop and take much further.

The first point to note about New Lanark is that it was a virgin site. Everything, the ingenious water lade system through a 100 yard tunnel from above Dundaff Linn, the road from Lanark, the four mills and eleven water wheels, and the village with its open areas and solid, unpretentious but sound tenements for housing the work force had to be built by Dale from scratch. The housing Braxfield Row (1790), the Double Row (1792), Caithness Row (1795) and the New Building (1798), is still immensely impressive.

The four mills contained some of the most technologically advanced design features of the period, including a warm air heating system. The largest mill, six storeys and 70' high with a frontage of 156', was the biggest cotton mill in the world for a time.

Robert Owen (1771-1858) took the management of the mills further in his drive to raise productivity and profitability. Under Owen from 1799/1800 to 1828/29 the mills produced some £300,000 in profits. Owen introduced better safety rules and restrictions to prevent wasteful accidents, more effective stock control and costing methods, checks on the performance of individual workers including the famous 'silent monitor', what would be called to-day a 'brand image' with pictures of New Lanark on bundles of yarn, facilities for cooking food during the lunch break, a compulsory fund with contributions deducted from wages to pay for the factory doctor and the care of the sick and injured, and New Lanark 'Summer Time' by which the clocks were put on by 30 minutes in the summer. Like Dale in 1786 so Owen in 1809 paid his workers their wages when a mill, had to close down temporarily. The main difference between Dale and Owen was that Owen introduced a ban on the employment of children under the age of 10.

New Lanark was for Owen an opportunity to try out a whole series of comprehensive experiments in social engineering and the education of children and adults on a totalitarian lifelong basis. He drew together ideas from France and Prussia and Eng-and and, with great skill, presented them as his own. Owen was also an indefatigable self-publicist, addressing meetings all over Britain and America, and producing an unending stream of articles and pamphlets and books, in particular *A New View of Society* (1812-13) and his *Report to the County of Lanark* (1820).

Owen's energy and enthusiasm were remarkable. He was

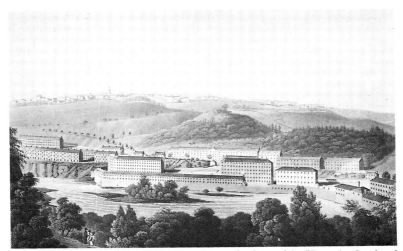

John H. Clark (1771-1863), New Lanark, from his *Views in Scotland* (1824). Clark probably visited New Lanark about 1820.

determined to create a contented, hard-working, clean, healthy, sober work force. He was, however, impatient of immediate success and particularly prone to making extravagant claims about the importance of his work for the future of New Lanark, for the British dominions and for every nation in the world. He was simultaneously proprietor, President, Prime Minister and Minister of Enlightenment and Culture of his own fiefdom.

Under Owen there was a whole war against dirt and disease including a private daily street cleaning and refuse collection service, paved streets, a washing-house and bleaching green, competitions for 'bug-free' houses, a patrol which checked out the cleanliness and sobriety of each household, and a women's committee which was responsible for visiting every house and publishing a weekly list of the best kept units. A register was kept of births and marriages and deaths. Fines were imposed for drunkenness and for having children outside the bonds of wedlock. Public houses in or near New Lanark were closed down.

A village store with bow windows was established in 1810 to sell goods, clothes, food, coal, and oddly also whisky, bought in bulk and sold at modest prices. The profits from the company store were re-invested in the school or other projects. The Institute for the Formation of Character (1816) and the School for Children

(1817), by any standard large and elegant semi-public buildings, housed a whole series of innovations in the education of children and adults. These included a nursery or infant school for babes aged 2, or younger, to 4; compulsory schooling for children up to the age of 10, and part-time evening classes for children between 10 and 12; the abolition of corporal punishment, and a curriculum with an emphasis on visual aids, coloured canvases, music, singing, dancing; and classes for adults, lecture rooms, a musicians' gallery, and supervised folk dancing and military drill every morning.

It was an encyclopaedic vision in which everyone, adults, children, were to have their lives organised from the cradle to the grave. It appeals particularly to those, industrialists, politicians, who share the view that working people are not capable of looking after their own affairs. It had little or no relevance to the real problems of the urban masses in nineteenth century Glasgow or Manchester or London. It was a magnificent Utopia.

CHAPTER 6

Canyon Clyde: Kirkfieldbank, Crossford, Carluke and Dalserf

From the falls at Corra Linn to the green plains beyond Dalserf the Clyde passes through a canyon with 200, 300, 400 feet high steep banks on each side of the river. The gorges at Corra Linn and Stonebyres are truly spectacular, but even they pale into a sort of insignificance compared to the ravine worn out by the Mouse Water at Cartland Craigs. The sheltered hillsides are covered with trees and rare shrubs and ferns and mosses and the more ordinary orchids and primroses and waves of bluebells, all listed in John Lightfoot's *Flora Scotica* (1777) and Roger Hennedy's *Clydesdale Flora* (1865, 1869, 1874, 1878, 1891). The slopes are by no means stable. The Braidwood-Crossford B7056 road and the Auchenglen road have both been closed in 1990-91 because of land slippage problems, and the main A72 from Lanark to Hamilton cut along the south side of the Clyde in the 1790s takes at times a very thin line between the river and the hill above.

The hillsides and the rich clay haughs or holm land in the bottom below became known in the last quarter of the nineteenth century as 'the orchard country' or 'the garden of Scotland'. Fruit farms and orchards and small holdings mushroomed from Kirkfieldbank, Hazelbank, Crossford and Rosebank to Dalserf, and on the north bank of the river from Nemphlar, Braidwood, Waygateshaw and Milton Lockhart to Garrion Bridge. A favourite Caledonian Railway excursion, especially popular in May and early June when the area was a blaze of white and pink blossoms, was to go from Glasgow to Lanark, then by coach to the Falls and 'Up the Clydeside' to Crossford, and then zigzag up to Tillietudlem Station near Craignethan Castle for the train back to Glasgow.

The tradition of fruit growing up the Clydeside may have had its origins in land use skills introduced and developed by the Tironensians at Lesmahagow Priory post 1144. Apples, pears, plums and gooseberries (or grozets) were being grown for the Glasgow auction market in largescale commercial enterprises by the late eighteenth century. James Scott, the minister in Carluke for example, mentions in the Statistical Accoaunt that there were

Kirkfieldbank – the old Clydesholm Bridge, 1695-99, and the new bridge with the A72.

for example, mentions in the Statistical Account that there were five miles of orchards and eighty acres of land in use for fruit in his parish in 1793. No fewer than forty eight varieties of apples and thirty two varieties of pears, subdivided into Summer, Harvest and Winter crops, were available.

Large scale planting of strawberries began in Hamilton, Blantyre and Uddingston *c.*1869/1878, and in Carluke by William Scott at Mashock Mill in 1872. Robert and William Scott's "Jelly Work" at Carluke "and the Glasgow market absorbed an immense tonnage of strawberries" and then raspberries and red, white and black currants. The best accounts of the Clydeside fruit orchards and fields are in A. MacCallum Scott's *Clydesdale* (1924), which includes a detailed picture of 'the orchard country' in the 1880s, and in Robert McLellan's *Linmill Stories* (1990) about his grandparents' fruit farm *c.*1912-22.

The whole business, digging, weeding, pruning, grafting, picking, weighing, sorting, packing, carting to market, was very labour intensive. At the height of the picking season some 2,000 women, children and men from Larkhall, Hamilton, Motherwell and even Glasgow were travelling to work each day. McLellan's stories are especially good with their descriptions of the Irish workers, the Donegals, living in barns and garrets, locked in after

80

10 o'clock at night, moving on from the strawberries to the Upper Ward farms for the hay and the 'tatties': and for his memories of the Dafties, Daft Sanny, Johnny Kirkhope, Joe the Pole, living and working on Linnmill, frightening off the crows with trays and porridge spurtles and carrying in baskets from the fields, looked over once a year by the man from the 'Coonty Cooncil.'

The era of the great tomato glasshouses, hundreds of acres of glistening factories for Clydeside Tomatoes, dates from mainly the post 1900s or even the 1920s.

The 1980s has been a period of decline with orchards and fruit fields and glasshouses lying empty or underutilised. On the positive side garden centres, for example at Sandyholm, with an emphasis on picking your own fruit, have flourished. Some glass-houses have become packing plants or banana ripening depots. Currently a new type of leisure centre with everything from miniature railways to swimming pools and ski slopes has been evolving at Kirkfieldbank and Crossford and crops of commuter housing have spread out from Carluke and Braidwood.

One idea which might have some real scientific value and could also attract thousands of amateur gardeners from a wide area, perhaps even from England, would be a fruit farm and orchard centre which specialised in rare varieties of fruits and berries from the nineteenth and eighteenth centuries. Would it be possible to see again and to sample the old plums, the Magnum Bonum, the Orleans, Burnets, Whithcorns, Horsejags? or the pears, the Jargonelle, Beurre, Hazel, Crawford, Achan, Good Christian, Muirfowl Egg, Lady's Thigh, Grey Guidwife, the Green Pear o' Pinkie? or the old apples, the Courpendu, Lass o' Gowrie, Colvilles, Fullwoods, Silver Saturday, Dumbarton Pippin, Hamilton Pippin, Orbiston, Summer and Winter Eli, Teuchat's Egg, Tam Montgomery, Leddingtons, the Blantyre Rennet or Dalziel Manse Codlin, Cam'nethan Pippin? or even some of the strawberries from the 1880s or the 1920s?

Cartland Craigs, Kirkfieldbank and Stonebyres

To explore this amazing corner follow the A73 road to one of Scotland's best-kept secrets, Cartland Bridge. Walk from Lanark or park in the lay-by on the west side of the road before Cartland Bridge Hotel or Baronald, built in 1890. The three arch bridge,

built in 1822-23 with Thomas Telford (1757-1834) overseeing
the work done locally by Mr Gibb, is one of the most splendid and
elegant constructions in Scotland. It spans the immense ravine
cut out by the Mouse Water 129' below. The tree cover obscures
most of this so it is a real shock to look over the south parapet and
discover the bridge for the firsts time.

   On the west side of the bridge a path to the right continues past
the site of a round structure, either a pavilion or a wartime gun
emplacement, climbing up to between 200' and 300' on Cartland
Craigs above the Mouse Water. Continue only as long as you feel
safe. The Castle Qua fort site (873449) may be mediaeval. No
access is possible to the "Wallace's Cave" in the ravine just north
of the bridge.

   From the west side of Cartland Bridge walk down the road to
the village of Kirkfieldbank, passing at the bottom the late
eighteenth or nineteenth century Mouse Mill and Mouse Mill
House on the west and east banks of the Mouse Water. Both are
on much earlier mediaeval sites. The romantically ruinous single
arch 'Roman Bridge' (869442) above the present bridge was
built in 1649.

   Cross to Kirkfieldbank using the old Clydesholm Bridge (1695-
99) with its fine solid round arches and piers. The modern bridge
opened in April 1959 is in its own way just as functional and
attractive.

   Kirkfieldbank developed round the mediaeval ferry at Clydesholm. Note the eighteenth and nineteenth century weavers'
cottages and the old orchards and fruit fields above the village.

   Regular bus services are available along Clydeside to Crossford
and Hamilton and back up the hill to Lanark. Drivers should
park their cars in the area beside the village hall and walk from
there to the Falls of Clyde at Stonebyres. Continue along the A72
passing the Strathclyde Regional Council Water Department
service bridge below the row of cottages formerly known as
Dublin and a crossing place in the river shallows. Take the
metalled road on the right at the bend before Linnville and
continue down to the weir above Stonebyres Falls. Cross the bridge
at the weir and follow the wide path above the north bank of the
river and the falls (852440). The three tiers in a narrow bedded
fall of about 60' has the sort of horrid savagery which impressed
Victorian visitors more than Corra Linn or Bonnington. The

The bridges at Kirfieldbank.

present path, however, does not provide a good view of the Falls.

The Nasmyth painting of Stonebyres shows the old lint mill (Linnmill) at the top of the Falls: note the flat site at the foot of the Linnmill parks at the Lowp where a foolish young man might just be able to jump across the Clyde. Continue on the path until it drops down to Stoneybyres Power Station. Retrace your steps to the weir and Kirkfieldbank or walk down to the power station and behind it and up to the A72 near Dark Bridge.

Cartland and Nemphlar

Cartland and Nemphlar were both small mediaeval villages. Each had its own pre-Reformation chapel, recalled in the latter by the site of Chapel Knowe and My Lady's Well on the West Nemphlar Road from Cartland Bridge to Nemphlar. Cartland became a short-lived 'parchment' burgh of barony in 1607.

These, and indeed most locations on the north side of the Clyde, are best explored on walking expeditions. Take a Carluke bus along the A73 to the Cartland Moor Road end. Walk up to Cartland and return to the main road. Turn right and after about fifty yards take the path on the south side of the road through the

Burgh Wood down to the driveway leading to Lee Castle: cross and continue along the rough road over the Mashock Burn to Lockhartbank and then uphill to the Nemphlar Moor Road and Nemphlar village. From Nemphlar either turn west for a long walk along Nemphlar Moor Road by Davity Wood, Burned Wood and Aaronshill Wood to Crossford with fine views over the Clydeside; or, go through Nemphlar by East (town of) Nemphlar and along the old trackway by "The Ditches" to come out on the Kirkfieldbank to Cartland Bridge road just above the Sunnyside road.

Lee Castle, built by Gillespie Graham in 1822 for Sir Norman McDonald Lockhart of Lee and Carnwath, is a picturesque Gothic fantasy with a square castellated tower and circular corner turrets. It incoporates earlier seventeenth century work. The Loccard/Lockhart family have held the estate from the twelfth century. The Lee Penny, a stone with some magical healing powers, Sir Walter Scott's *Talisman*, was collected by Sir Symon Loccard when crusading against the Moors in Spain.

For another view of Lee Castle from the distance walk down Auchenglen Road off the A73 at Braidwood just beyond the Heads Point Nursery Centre. Continue down the road east of the Fiddler Burn and Samson's Slingsteps passing the converted west gatehouse or lodge entrance to the Castle policies, Auchenglen farm and the site of St Oswald's Chapel above the west bank of the burn opposite the farm. Continue by Burnbank and Birkhill to the Crossford Sewage Trestment Plant and Crossford Bridge.

Hazelbank and Lesmahagow

After Stonebyres Power Station the Clyde runs merrily on its way below the Linn Burn and Poplar Park and Stonebyres Low Wood to the cliffs at Arthur's Craigs and Hazelbank. McLellan has a lovely account of hunting for "beirdies" (like minnows but with whiskers!) at the Carlin Stane half a mile downriver from Stonebyres. On it a mermaid was said to sit combing her yellow hair.

Every September the river from Hazelbank Park to Sandyholm beyond Crossford is enlivened by the annual Raft Race. Over £44,000 has been raised for Scottish and local charities in these fun runs over the last eleven years. The 1990 race had eightyseven entries on rafts ranging in shape and style from funeral parties

Cartland Craigs Bridge (1822) over the Mouse Water. Designed by Thomas Telford and still part of the A73 today. Note in the print by T. Allom the typical washday sequence at the left.

and orchestras to racing cars. Each competitor pays £3 for the opportunity of drowning or breaking an arm or leg. Spectators seem to be encouraged to pelt them with flour bombs and eggs. No doubt it has all been shown on Japanese television screens as an example of traditional Scottish life.

Hazelbank is a spaciously laid out village with houses with goodsized gardens and old orchards climbing up the hillside behind. The de Veres' Stonebyres House, a Victorian baronial edifice of 1840 with additions in 1906-14, was demolished in 1934.

Circuit the area by taking the B7018 from Linnville on the A72 up to the National Trust for Scotland viewpoint on Blackhill fort and returning by Hallhill and the A744 to Hazelbank. The large Iron Age hill fort contains a Bronze Age cairn. At 951' the views, possibly even to Arran and Ben Lomond, are spectacular.

The B7018 to Lesmahagow is a lively short drive by car. Lesmahagow, down in its own valley by the Nethan, was essentially until recently a small mining town or village. It has, however, a long and interesting history as the centre of the Tironensian priory established by David I in 1144 and colonised from Kelso. The priory was richly endowed with an annual income from lands at Draffan and at Little Kype near Strathaven and the church at Kilmaurs. Excavations in the late 1970s on the site to the south of the present parish church (1803) revealed the foundations of the west range and cloister walk and the frater. The church, dedicated to St Machutus, was possibly on a much earlier Christian site with a special sanctity attached to it and with four crosses marking out the precinct as a sanctuary.

Crossford and Craignethan

The fords from the Cross Ford, the Smugglers Ford at Nethanfoot, Threepwood, Milton and Maudslie to Dalserf became less important after the bridge at Crossford, the most central crossing point along the Clydeside between Lanark and Hamilton, was opened in 1793. In the fruit era the Holm Land and the Nethan valley behind were the home of a large number of orchards and glasshouses. The published collections of letters from Gavin Scott of Hillend, Crossford, to his son George, a medical officer in Malaysia, provide a fascinating picture of local life, the fruit farm economy, the tomato growers, the sale of the trees in Carfin Wood in January 1915 at two shillings and sixpence per tree, harvesting accidents and deaths from diptheria, and of local scandals, for example the marriage of a woman aged 64 to her foreman aged 30. To date the letters from 1911 to 1915 have been edited and privately published by Ruth Richens in Cambridge (1981-90) under the title *Your Loving Father, Gavin Scott. Letters from a Lanarkshire Farmer.*

In the 1990s the Clyde Valley Country Estate project with plans for car parking facilities, walkways, a bowling green, the restoration of the old iron suspension footbridge over the Clyde near Carfin and a narrow gauge railway along the river is likely to be successful. It may, however, therefore significantly add to the already serious traffic congestion problems along the A72 during the peak summer months.

The Nethan Gorge Scottish Wildlife Trust Reserve and Craignethan Castle are two major sites visited from Crossford. The Gorge footpath begins on the north side of the A72 road bridge (823470) over the River Nethan just after the road signposted to the castle. It takes about half an hour to follow the path up along the gorge through the protected native broadleaved

Nemphlar in the winter.

woodland, along the edge of a field and then down into the hollow north of the castle before finally climbing up to the outer courtyard area. The O.S. 6" scale map *c*.1859 marks a coal pit (820466) on the south side of the Nethan. Another remnant of the old great wood can be seen at Townhead along the Ponfeigh Burn (888356) near Rigside.

Craignethan (or Draffane) Castle is an absolute showpiece, a one-off example of the most modern sixteenth century dirty tricks in military architecture and the uses of artillery. It was built between 1530 and 1540 by Sir James Hamilton of Finnart, the illegitimate son of the 1st Earl of Arran who was the grandson of James II. Sir James was a remarkable man, a Scottish-French Renaissance scholar, architect and master of works to the royal palaces, a business tycoon and salesman and shrewd speculator in land and property, above all a great show-off with a fine sense of humour. It is little wonder that he was executed in 1540 for suspected treason against James V. His Craignethan was an exercise in building for pleasure and display, an opportunity for him to display all his skills and expertise. After his death Craignethan passed to his half-brother James Hamilton, 2nd Earl of Arran and later (in 1549) Duke of Chatelherault. Four

Crossford Raft Race September 1990. A three-mile fun run down the rapids from Crossford to Sandyholm. To make it more difficult the contestants are pelted with flour bombs and eggs! The 1990 event raised £4000 used to sponsor four guide dogs for the blind: other beneficiaries included the Epilepsy Association of Scotland, the Multiple Sclerosis Society and Ridgepark House for Autistic Children. (*Lanarkshire Gazette* photograph).

years after his death in 1575 the castle was demolished and cast down by order of the Privy Council. The new range of buildings in the outer courtyard was built by Andrew Hay who purchased Craignethan in 1659.

The castle of 1530-40 was a highly sophisticated and scholarly fortification behind a massive curtain wall placed behind and above a deep rock cut ditch. Across the ditch lay the amazing caponier, rediscovered in 1962, a sort of fortified passageway sunk into the ditch so that it could be raked with gunfire from the wide-mouthed loopholes. The curtain wall and the south-east corner tower carried an extraordinary series of gunports for defence by small cannon and handguns. Note in particular the sloping gunports in the south-east or Kitchen Tower.

The main residence, the tower house, is exceptionally spacious and palatial, planned for comfort and warmth: note the wide stairways. The great joke, of course, was that all the display of gunports and defences were of little real use because the castle, although virtually impossible to attack from the north or east or

Hallbar or Braidwood Tower.

south, is overlooked on the west by a high plateau from which the whole area could be ravaged by heavy cannon in any serious engagement. Arguably this heavy artillery was not available in Scotland until after 1547-49, but Hamilton himself with his knowledge of French and Italian seigecraft was surely well aware of impending changes.

Return from Craignethan by the road running west from the castle to the old railway line and the station at Tillietudlem. The latter name comes from Sir Walter Scott who set a number of the episodes in *Old Mortality* in what was very clearly Craignethan. Turn down the hill to the Nethan at Holm Land, crossing the river by the green iron bridge by Alex. Findlay & Co. of Parkneuk Bridge Works in Motherwell to the old glasshouses at Corramill: continue up the very steep zigzag hill to the Hallhill to Crossford road for some very fine views across to the glasshouses above the Clyde. Take the hedged lane directly down into Crossford to the

War Memorial and the parish church. This road to and from Crossford is suitable for cars, and can take even a fifteen seater minibus, but great caution is required and some first gear work is necessary on the hairpin bends.

Braidwood, Maudslie and Carluke

It is also convenient to explore the north bank of the Clyde from Crossford. The B7056 Braidwood Road passes the site of Mashock Mill (834467) on the Mashock Burn below: note the old coal mines east of Braidwood Road at 846471 north of St. Oswald's Chapel and west of the road at 833471 off the side road to Linnside and Swinsy Hill. Hallbar Tower (840470) is a late fifteenth or early sixteenth century tower house built by either Alex. Stewart post 1482 or the Earl of Arran post 1497. It was purchased by the Lockharts in 1681. The tower, altered and repaired in 1581 and 1861, is 58' high with a flagstone roof and 24'8" square with 5' thick walls. Each floor consists of one room with access from floor to floor by a steep and narrow intramural stairway.

The minor road by Linnside, Poplarglen, Gills and Waygateshaw to Meadowhead and Milton Road up to Carluke has fine views over to Threepwood and Sandyholm. There is another tower house and also a dovecot at Waygateshaw. General William Roy, whose work in mapping and trigonometrical surveying led to the foundation of the Ordnance Survey service, was born at Milton-head. A trigonometrical point and plaque, if not currently vandalised, marks his birthplace (825495). Yolande O'Donoghue's study of *William Roy 1726-1790* published by the British Library in 1977 includes, very appropriately, a full page reproduction of the section of *The Military Survey of Scotland* (*c.*1752-53) with Dalserf, Maudslie, Miltonhead and Sandyholm.

The site of Milton Lockhart House above a deep ravine west of Miltonhead was selected by Sir Walter Scott as a suitable location for a house for his son-in-law, John Gibson Lockhart. The house itself was dismantled four years ago and shipped to Japan to be re-assembled as part of a children's fantasy world on Hokkaido Island. The private access bridge over the Clyde near Overton was not exported to Japan.

In Carluke itself follow the A73 towards the centre of the town. Take the by-pass road signposted for the A721 to Peebles.

Carluke High Mill, December 1990. Built in the 1790s on the Black Mount above Carluke by David Dick.

Continue left ahead at the first and straight ahead at the second roundabout. Carluke High Mill on the Black Mount on the right is an important example of a windmill tower. The 32' high tower, originally of course with sails, was built *c.*1795 by David Dick. It is 27' diameter at ground level. The mill was converted to steam power in the 1830s and then to gas pre 1914. The buildings to the right of the tower include storage accommodation and the grain drying kiln. Milling ended about 1930. The High Mill Trust is gradually restoring the complex as a heritage and visitor centre. The Carluke Parish Historical Society is also a very active local group.

    Carluke or Kirkstyle became a burgh of barony in 1662. The

The hogback stone, Dalserf Churchyard.

church was probably flourishing in the earlier village sometime in the fifteenth or sixteenth century. The old church had fallen into disrepair by the end of the eighteenth century and the new church of St Andrews was built in 1799 to a design provided by Henry Bell, the steamboat engineer and inventor. The old walled churchyard at the first roundabout includes some interesting funerary monuments and fragments of the old churches.

The mediaeval and earlier church for the parish (Eglismale-soch) was located on the flat land close to the river in the Forest of Maudslie. It was still referred to in 1574 as the Forest Kirk. The large mound to the north-east may have been a motte and the site is mentioned in Blind Harry's epic poem of Wallace's life.

Maudslie Castle, which was built by the 5th Earl of Hyndford to plans by Robert Adam in 1792/93, was demolished in 1935. The private bridge over the Clyde to Rosebank was erected in 1861. Rosebank itself developed as a village for employees on the Maudslie estate.

Dalserf

Dalserf lies at the edge of the Lanarkshire coalfield. In the middle of the nineteenth century the nearest collieries at Over

Dalserf, Auldton and Cornsilloch were literally only two minutes walk up the hill from the village and the main road. In contrast the rich flat holm land was orchard country. Dalserf village itself slumbered through the last two hundred years like a Scottish Lowland Brigadoon. In the eighteenth century the village was a busy place with a major ferryboat operating across the Clyde near the church. There were five alehouses in the village up from the Boathouse north of the church. However the new turnpike road along the Clyde in the late 1790s, the opening of Garrion Bridge in 1818, and the opposition of the estate proprietor to encouraging any new building or granting any new leases or feus left Dalserf in peace.

As a result it is an idyllic corner, perfection. The old weavers' cottages have been restored. The parish church of M'Achanshire, from an Irish sixth century missionary saint, is an outstanding example of a small country Presbyterian building. It dates back to 1655, but is probably on an earlier site. Below the clock and spire on the south-east side of the church is the eleventh century hogback stone found on the site in 1897.

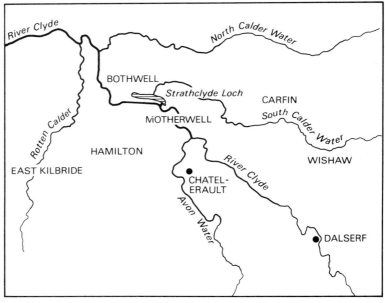

Dalserf to Bothwell Bridge.

CHAPTER 7

The Playing Fields: Chatelherault, Hamilton and Motherwell

From Garrion Bridge to Bothwell Bridge the Clyde meanders slowly, even sedately, through an area of vast contrasts. On the north bank between Garrion and Cambusnethan is the old orchard country, Pathhead, Wemysshill, Carbarnswood, Randalls and Kirkhill. On the south and west side the old coal pits at Cornsilloch, Skellyton, Larkhall, Merryton, Allanton, Dikehead Bog, Ferniegair and Haugh-head are only a distant memory, but their visible legacy of floodprone wetlands and subsidence problems remains. Hamilton still retains something of the grandiose elegance to be expected in a county town virtually at the gates of the palaces and courts of the eighteenth and nineteenth century Dukes of Hamilton, whereas on the other side of the Clyde are the brooding towers of the gradually expiring steel works and the municipal socialism of Motherwell and Wishaw. The ducal playing fields at Chatelherault on the west are balanced by the huge modern boating pond at Strathclyde Country Park. Close to the river on the haughs and holms are the remains of older civilizations, the early and mediaeval church sites at Cambusnethan and Dalziel and Hamilton Low Parks and the Roman fort and road and bath-house at Bothwellhaugh; and concealed behind are the spectacular gorges cut out by the Avon and, to a lesser extent, by the South Calder.

The crossroads of the A71 and the A72 at Garrion Bridge (1818) is a very busy junction. Just above the bridge on the north bank was the famous Garrion Mill which was still producing Camnethan Oats at the time of the compilation of the Third Statistical Account of Lanarkshire in the 1950s. A series of mills had been on the same site since at least the twelfth century, when it was worked on behalf of the Tironensians of Kelso Abbey. Garrion Tower nearby or its predecessor was a summer residnce of the fifteenth and sixteenth century Bishops of Glasgow and of their post-Reformation Episcopalian successors.

Cambusnethan and Dalziel

Like Maudslie and Dalserf the old churches of Cambusnethan (768540) and Dalziel (754550) were on flat haugh land close to the Clyde. Cross shafts have been found at each site. The churches, dedicated respectively to St Nethan and St Patrick, were both very early, possibly sixth or seventh or eighth century foundations. Cambusnethan (Kambusnaythan) churchyard is off Kirkhill Road which runs south from Netherton Road: it contains the mausoleums of the Belhaven and Stenton, the Stewart of Coltness and the Lockhart of Castlehill families. Dalziel churchyard, in the grounds of Dalzell Park west of Dalzell House, was the burial place of the Dalzells and the Hamiltons of Boggs. The former manse of 1827 to 1833 just north of the churchyard has very fine views across to the Barons Haugh Reserve.

Upriver Cambusnethan House or Priory (the 'priory' is a nineteenth century romantic affectation) east of the Gowkthrapple Burn is a Gothic creation of 1819-20 by Gillespie Graham for Robert Lockhart of Castlehill. Since 1945 it has been variously a private house, an architect's office, and a pseudo-mediaeval banqueting hall. The view over the river is quite splendid, but at the moment the house is a burnt out and vandalised shell. It is on the Scottish Civic Trust 'Buildings at Risk' list.

In contrast Dalzell House in Motherwell's Dalzell Park, directly south of the Fir Park football ground, has been restored recently and converted into eighteen private flats. The oldest part, a late fifteenth or sixteenth century Dalzell family tower house, is flanked on the south by a wing added by James Hamilton of Boggs c.1647-49. The 1857 north wing with its own confection of towers and turrets and battlement walks was the work of Robert W. Billings (1813-74), the eminent architectural historian and author of *The Baronial and Ecclesiastical Antiquities of Scotland* (1848-52). Billings also added a terraced garden above the Dalzell Burn imitating Barncluth and Edzell.

Dalzell House is a success story, fully justifying the use of the £500,000 "including £190,000" from Historic Buildings and Monuments, paid over in grants. Its main claim to importance, however, is not the building itself but the unique, the superb seventeenth century wooden panelling, including a panel of 1613, in the old great hall, the library, the minstrels' hall and the

The Clyde near Cambusnethan.

staircase well. It is indeed 'a source of constant regret', as was pointed out by David Emery and Ginny Kemp in a television programme, 'Making History Pay', shown on Channel 4 in March 1991, that no public access was arranged to at least some of these rooms in spite of the public money spent on Dalzell House as a whole.

The Royal Society for the Protection of Birds wetland reserve at Barons Haugh lies west of Dalzell House. The entrance (755552) is by a lane from North Lodge Avenue. Access is best arranged by contacting the RSPB warden. Barons Haugh, which has marsh and causeway hides, is likely to have a bird population of well over a thousand with very large numbers of teal, coot, mallard, wigeon and pochard and perhaps twenty cormorants. The area on both sides of the river, a sort of Clydesdale Camargue, is an ornithologist's paradise. The watery ponds and fields on the south-west bank at Merryton and Carbarns are grazing and resting areas for whooper swans: unfortunately the power cables between the pylon towers at Netherton and Ferniegair are a hazard which kills a number of swans every year. Strathclyde Country Park Loch also has some mute swans. Cormorants and kingfishers are especially interesting and herons from a heronry on the Hamilton racecourse side of the river. The west river bank

near the Clyde Bridge and the Mausoleum also includes more
nature reserve areas.

Cadzow and Chatelherault

The early church and centre of Cadzow (later Hamilton)
parish was on the flat haugh land where the Cadzow Burn joins
the Clyde, i.e. near the motte to the north of Hamilton Mausoleum
(1845-56) close to the M74. The castle of Cadihou in the twelfth
and thirteenth centuries was this motte. The 1450-51 collegiate
church of Hamilton, largely demolished in the 1730s by the 5th
Duke of Hamilton, was built on the land to the south-west of the
mausoleum on what became in the late sixteenth century the
grounds of the first Hamilton Palace. Hamilton itself became a
burgh of barony in 1456.

Cadzow Castle (734537) in Chatelherault Country Park on a
very dramatic situation 200' above the Avon was probably
developed by the Hamiltons in the later fourteenth or fifteenth
century. The crumbling cliff face is now extremely dangerous
and the castle can only be seen from outside secure fencing. The
two low round towers of c.1530-40 which were built into each end
of the rock-cut ditch were designed for a formidable battery of
artillery using wide-mouthed gunloops. There is a sort of frenetic
ingenuity and expertise about Cadzow which suggests the fine
hand of Sir James Hamilton of Finnart; alternatively the towers
may be the work of the 2nd Earl of Arran who was made Duc de
Chatellerault by Henri II of France in1548. The castle, in which
Mary Queen of Scots stayed in 1568, was dismantled by the
Regent Morton in 1579. Cadzow, like Craignethan, was seen as
dangerous just because it was so sophisticated, so innovative. It is
important as a Scottish example of artillery fortification belonging
to roughly the same period as Henry VIII's forts at Deal and
Walmer.

Chatelherault (pronounce as 'Shatt-ell-err-o', or more colloqu-
ially as 'Shattly Row' or 'The Wham') Country Park includes the
ducal "Dogg Kennells" or hunting lodge acquired for the nation
in 1968, 370 acres along the Avon gorges purchased in 1978 with
money from the National Land Fund and 138 acres in the Deer
Park added in 1985 from the National Heritage Memorial Fund.
Since 1979 over £7 million has been invested in restoration and
development projects at Chatelherault. The main entry is off the

Chatelherault in 1956.

A72 Larkhall and Lanark bus route; the old railway line by Allanton and Merryton to Larkhall should be reopened to provide easier access.

The first plans for the modern development of the High Parks were part of a whole grand design for new plantations and gardens and enclosures and avenues which originated with the 3rd Duke and the Duchess Anne (1656-1716) in the last quarter of the seventeenth century. The plans prepared by Alexander Edwards before his death in 1708 were taken much further by her grandson, the 5th Duke, who employed William Adam (1689-1748) on various projects on his Scottish estates between 1727 and 1743.

A three mile long formal avenue from Bothwell Bridge and Hamilton Palace ran up to the new skyline feature, Chatelherault, which was visible, as it still is to-day, for miles around. It was built between 1732 and 1744 to plans prepared by William Adam. He referred in his *Vitruvius Scoticus* to the new Baroque Palladian French chateau as the "Dogg Kennells at Hamilton". The dogs incidentally were to be clumber spaniels. Chatelherault was a sumptuous, ostentatious extravagance: at once a delight and a party place and retreat and a working kennels and hunting lodge.

The 280' long facade, with a profusion of urns and ball finials, incorporates four pink pavilion towers. The two at the north-east end were to provide accommodation for the gamekeepers and the gardeners; at the north-west end were the ducal apartments and the banqueting hall with exquisite cream and rose and amber plasterwork by his 'stuccetorian', the excellent Thomas Clayton. Behind the facade lay the terraced garden above the gorge, the bowling green, and the courtyard with stables, kennels, coach-house and offices. The courtyard was used in the 1750s for a more exotic purpose as a sort of menagerie for monkeys, baboons, wolves, leopards and bears. Perhaps fortuitously the bear pit being prepared in the garden for the polar bears was not ready when they arrived at Leith in 1753.

The north-west pavilions were damaged by a fire in 1946 and the whole building was thoroughly vandalised in the late 1960s. It was literally a roofless shell by 1977. In addition there were problems with mining subsidence and with largescale sand quarrying in the Deer Park close to the lodge. Only a few fragments of the interior work had survived the ravages of the last years. The restoration programme between 1979 and 1987 has been an enormous success. Stone from the original quarry nearby was used for repairs to the external fabric, and miracles have been achieved taking old photographs as a guide for using synthetic materials to recreate Thomas Clayton's plasterwork. The panoply of classical deities, Bacchus, Pan, Apollo, Luna, Vulcan, Venus, Ceres and Diana, the goddess of hunting, in the banqueting hall and the Duke's Apartment is quite breathtaking. The hall is let out for occasional functions and receptions.

The terraced garden is being recreated as it might have been in the 1740s with a formal parterre and clipped box hedges and yew uprights and a maze of little paths. The Visitor Centre with tableaux of the miners, the woodcutters, the gardeners, the huntsmen who worked for the Dukes of Hamilton in the eighteenth century is very well done.

The Country Park is laid out in a series of walks and routes. The most important first exploration is across the Duke's Bridge over the Avon to Cadzow Castle, and then south-west passing the slight remains of an Iron Age fort to the old oaks in the High Parks. The 300 oak trees have amassed an enormous girth since they were planted in the fifteenth century. The wild white cattle with their blaçk eyes and ears and muzzles originally wandered through the mediaeval hunting forest. Their descendants are now penned in the deer park below Chatelherault. They may look docile, but it is worth remembering that they are wild animals, not just rather large Herefords! If facing aggressors, and these could be just boys chasing a football, they might form up in a straight line and decide to look after themselves. The original Chatelherault herd was exterminated about 1760 "for economical reasons". Had they chased the wolves or the leopards?

The Avon gorges between Barncluth, Cadzow, the Avon Braes and Fairholm Bridge north of Larkhall are up to 200' deep through sandstone with some limestone and coal seams. Look out for herons, foxes, badgers, squirrels, carpets of wild flowers and masses of rare fungi and toadstools. One footpath follows the route of an early horse drawn mineral railway to Howlet Row passing the site of the old coal pit (736531) at Avonbank.

The chain of footpaths can be followed south to Green Bridge and Fairholm Bridge and the B7078 to Larkhall, or south-west to Millheugh and Larkhall. The Broomhill viaduct (754503) 170' above the Avon south of Millheugh was built by the Arrol Brothers in 1904 for the Caledonian Railway. The most interesting recent development in Larkhall itself was the opening in 1990 of the Guide Dogs for the Blind Association training centre in Macpherson House in Hamilton Street, the first in the West of Scotland area.

North of Chatelherault the footpaths continue to the three span seventeenth century Old Avon Bridge. The Avon Bridge to the east was built to plans by Thomas Telford in 1820: the viaduct to the west carrying the Hamilton-Motherwell line was built in 1860 for the Caledonian Railway. On the west the footpath continues from Cadzow by the Duke's Monument, a Greek temple erected for the 11th Duke who died in 1863, to Barncluth Road in Hamilton.

The private grounds at Barncluth conceal a fine late sixteenth or seventeenth century tower house, an elegant eighteenth century garden pavilion ('the old Hamilton court-house'), and remarkable seventeenth century hanging gardens in a series of steep terraces above the Avon. A few tantalising glimpses are available from the railway line into Hamilton from Motherwell.

Hamilton to Motherwell: The Walk

Starting from Motherwell Railway Station take the train to Hamilton Central. This short journey, which includes the 80' high Camp viaduct over the Clyde with a fine vista east over to Barons Haugh, a tunnel, and the viaduct over the Avon before Barncluth, is a delight. British Rail, the current owners of the track and operators of the service, should really go out of their way to market it as a scenic route, a small local equivalent to the West Highland line at Arisaig and Beasdale.

At Hamilton Central across the bus terminal area and continue down Leechlee Road, the route to the M74. On the left is William Adam's Old Parish Church commissioned by the 5th Duke in 1732 to replace the mediaeval collegiate church. Alterations in 1842 and 1926, including the cupola over the crossing, have not essentially spoiled the church which has a circular body with four cross aisles. The Netherton Cross in front of the church was brought there in 1926 from its earlier location some 60 yards from the motte in the Low Parks near the Mausoleum. It probably belongs to the eighth or ninth century. Note the whirling disc symbol (also found at Govan), the interlacing, the fishes and the presumably biblical scenes with human figures. The Heads Memorial in the east wall of the churchyard, a highlight of the local Covenanters Trail, commemorates four local men executed after the 1666 Pentland Rising.

Turn left along Cadzow Street. The Library opened by Andrew Carnegie in 1907 has a fine collection of local books and archives. Note the spectacular display case on the first floor with two of the Cadzow white cattle. The adjacent District Council or Municipal Buildings are dated 1914. Turn right down Muir Street by the Town Hall (1926) and right again at the bottom of the hill for the Hamilton District Museum, formerly the Hamilton Arms Inn (1696). The museum, which has an active publications record, includes excellent sections dealing with local coal mining, transport and farm equipment, hand-loom weaving and lace-making, and Sir Harry Lauder's music hall costumes. The eight-eenth century Assembly Room has been restored to its original condition in coaching days.

Directly behind the District Museum in the former ducal riding school is the Cameronian Museum. It has a really fascinating collection of militaria, uniforms, medals, trophies, paintings and photographs, eminently clearly and attractively displayed.

Continue across the Low Parks with the Lanarkshire Ice Rink and Hamilton Racecourse (1888) on the left to the Mausoleum built as a crypt and chapel by and for the 10th Duke, Alexander (1767-1852). The principal architect was David Bryce. This strange monument to human pride and folly, and above all pomposity, was built between 1845 and 1856. The dome is 120' high. The building imitates the Castle of St Angelo in Rome: the 1½ ton bronze doors are a copy taken from the Baptistry in Florence. The disastrous fifteen second echo, which made the building quite hopeless as a chapel, and the marble mosaic floors are other features of possible interest.

The Mausoleum has sunk some 18' because of mining subsidence, not sufficient to require its demolition. Note the glorious sleepy lions by Alexander H. Ritchie.

The most perfect piece of bad taste was the purchase of an Egyptian basalt sarcophagus which the 10th Duke intended to use as his coffin. It was only discovered on his deathbed that it was too small for him: or perhaps nobody had dared to mention such an inconsiderate fact to him previously. Supposedly his last words were "Double me up".

The Mausoleum was the largest object of its kind in Scotland. Similarly Hamilton Palace was at the very top of the league of super colossal private houses. The early palace of 1591 and 1705 was converted by the 10th Duke in the 1820s and 1830s into a massive edifice with a 265' long and 60' high frontage, reverting here to plans suggested by William Adam. The 120' long gallery and the vast rooms were adorned with paintings by Reubens and Titian and Velasquez and furniture from Versailles. The 10th Duke had prudently enhanced his already vast wealth by marrying his cousin Susan Beckford in 1810, which placed him (using twentieth century terms) in the Getty or Mellon class. The seventeen day sale of paintings and furniture and treasures from Hamilton Palace in 1882 realised the enormous sum of £397,562.

The 12th Duke, a gambler and spendthrift on the grand scale, began an extended programme of coalmining and sandquarrying into the Low Parks area. The subsidence problems that led to the demolition of the Palace by the Town Council between 1922 and 1927 probably began with this slightly careless enthusiasm for more easy profits. The village of Bothwellhaugh beside the

Hamilton Park Colliery is now under the water of Strathclyde Loch.

From the Mausoleum continue south-east of the twelfth century motte close to the M74, through the underpass and then across the footbridge over the Clyde towards the Watersports Centre at the end of Strathclyde Loch. The artificial loch with facilities for waterski-ing, rowing, canoeing and sailing is the centrepiece of the 1,650 acre Strathclyde Country Park opened in 1978.

Cross the weir at the south-east end of the loch and continue along the shore of the loch along the east and north bank. After passing the north end of the island close to the shore take the path up the hill to the plateau above the Clyde and the South Calder (731578), the site of the four acre second century Antonine period Bothwellhaugh Roman fort. A few sections of the ramparts are just barely visible at the south-east of the fort, which was recorded as far back as the Statistical Account in 1792. The fort was excavated in 1938-39 and 1967-68.

The Roman rest and relaxation bath-house found during the period when the loch was being prepared in 1973 was excavated in 1975-76 and then dismantled and rebuilt between 1979 and 1981 on its present site. The various rooms are clearly labelled, the furnace room, the hot room, the warm room, the cold bath plunge and the cold room.

Continue across the South Calder by the modern bridge. The 'Roman' bridge, ironically and coincidentally close to the line of the Roman road, is a seventeenth century packhorse bridge. Just north of the bridge in the South Calder valley is another 'Wallace's Cave', all very reminiscent of the Mouse and Cartland Bridge near Lanark.

Turn off to the right before Bothwellhaugh Road up the hill through the woods on the high ground west of the South Calder Water below. (An alternative would be to arrange for a car to collect you here and continue by the Fun Fair and Visitor Centre and the A725 to Bothwell Bridge and Blantyre.) The footpath goes through the grounds of Orbiston House, the site in 1825 of one of Robert Owen's unsuccessful experimental schemes. Continue on the path bearing east along the side of the golf course above the South Calder, noting the rectangular seventeenth century dovecot tower on the right. The path swings north-west and over the main Glasgow to London railway line to

Sir George Reid, Bothwell Bridge (1886).

Fairways and Community Road on the edge of the Orbiston council housing estate. This route provides a fine view across to the last of the great steel works over to the east. From Community Road take a Kelvin Central service bus into Motherwell by the A721 through Forgewood to the Railway Station.

Near the station the Byzantine tower and nave (1915) of the former Dalziel Free or United Free or North Church, now the G.L.O. Centre, houses a coffee and book shop. The building, splendidly maintained, has a superbly functional rectangular nave with a very Byzantine round domed roof and round pillars.

It is not easy to see what the future holds for Motherwell and its satellite villages. As a steel town rapidly running out of steel workers it is losing its very reason for existence. In the 1870s and 1880s it began a period of rapid expansion with workers and their families arriving not only from the rest of Lowland Scotland and the nine counties of Ulster but also from Poland and Lithuania. The coal mines, the iron and steel works have virtually all gone, vanished or vanishing into oral tradition.

The railway journey from Glasgow to Edinburgh via Holytown and Carfin and Cleland and Hartwood and Shotts should be a compulsory exercise for all Scots really interested in the future and welfare of the people of Scotland. To lift the depression stop off at Carfin halt to visit St. Xavier R.C. Church (1881) and the Grotto opened in 1925. It is now a place of summer pilgrimmage for thousands of the faithful and the hopeful from all over Scotland. The Grotto, with its garden and streams in honour of Sister Therese of the Child Jesus at Lourdes, was built by Father Taylor and a group of out-of-work miners and helpers. Perhaps some miracles are possible after all.

CHAPTER 8

Bothwell, Low Blantyre and Uddingston

Bothwell

After the plains of Bothwellhaugh, the banks of the River Clyde close in again at Bothwell Bridge, a geographical feature which historically gave it strategic importance as a crossing point. Until 1650 this was the first bridge downstream across the Clyde. On the north side of the bridge is a monument to the memory of the Covenanting forces who suffered a heavy defeat here at the hands of the Royalist Highland Army of the Duke of Monmouth. The events immediately leading up to this battle had started on May 3rd 1679 when the unpopular Archbishop James Sharp of St. Andrews had been dragged from his coach on Magus Muir and murdered by a band of Covenanters, led by John Balfour of Kinloch. The Government decided that ruthless action had to be taken and they raised an army to put down the rebellion. On June 22nd confident after a small victory over the Royalists at Drumclog, the Covenanters were camped on the south bank of the Clyde at Bothwell, holding possession of the Bridge itself. At that time, the bridge was very narrow, and sloped steeply up towards the centre.

A small contingent of 300 men, led by David Hackston and Hall of Haughhead defended the bridge against the attack of the Royalist Army from the north. The Covenanters were pushed back to the south bank where a bloody battle ensued. The Covenanters were routed: 400 were killed; over 1200 were taken prisoner, many of whom were later executed. The brutality of the King's troops during that year has left us a legacy of sympathetic affection for the Covenanters and their martyrs which their own conduct does not merit. Their military actions had been just as violent and merciless, including a massacre of all their prisoners, men, women and children by General Leslie after the Battle of Philiphaugh in 1645.

Bothwell Bridge today is the 17th century bridge widened and improved twice in the 19th century, in 1826 and 1871. The bridge has four spans with ribbed arches and triangular cutwaters to

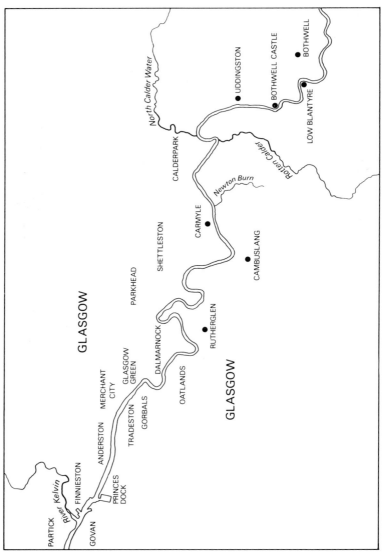

Bothwell Bridge to Glasgow.

The Georgian architecture of the Anchorage, c.1805, Bothwell.

cope with the force of water as the river narrows.

Immediately north of the Bridge lies Bothwell, now essentially a residential village where most of the inhabitants travel outwith the area to work. Its centre lies around the church of St. Brides whose red square tower is a landmark for miles around. It is believed that there may have been a chapel on this site since the 6th century, and fragments unearthed during the reconstruction of the church in 1933 are certainly evidence of a 12th century Norman building. In the 14th century the Gothic choir which survives today was added by Archbishop the Grim, 3rd Earl of Douglas. The western end of the church was rebuilt in the 19th century to a design by the architect David Hamilton, who was responsible for many other notable buildings including Hutcheson's Hospital and Glasgow Royal Exchange. After this the Gothic choir was no longer used, and fell into disrepair, until on the 500th anniversary of its foundation, it was beautifully restored by Sir Rowand Anderson. However the 'old' and 'new' churches remained separate until 1933 when they were united into a beautiful and atmospheric whole.

The 19th century building is Late Decorated Perpendicular Gothic and has unusual carvings of local celebrities over the windows. Some on the south side have been identified as Meg Steel, one time landlady of the nearby Douglas Arms, William Allan, the school teacher, and James Watson the gravedigger. The square tower is stacked in three layers with pinnacles at each corner, looking rather like an architectural wedding cake. The Gothic choir has a remarkable stone roof, one of the few of its kind in Scotland, covered in large stone slabs, each weighing 2 cwts. The total weight of the roof slabs is therefore 100 tons. Inside, this roof is supported by an unusual pointed barrel vault. The east end is almost entirely filled with a beautiful stained glass window designed by Sir Edward Burne-Jones, depicting the Nativity, and its rich colours bathe the interior. The medieval atmosphere is perhaps rather spoilt by two enormous monuments to local aristocracy, which dominate the small choir. One is a French made memorial to the Third Duke of Hamilton (1634-94) which was brought from the Old Kirk of Hamilton to its present site when the church was demolished in 1852. The other monument is to the Earls of Douglas who named this church after their patron saint, St. Bride. The church is still surrounded by its graveyard, and has some interesting gravestones set amidst laurels and yew trees. There are two separate entrances to the church grounds. To the east is the Dixon Entrance, gifted by James S. Dixon, a member of the congregation who also donated the tower clock and chimes. Further west is the Donald Entrance beside which is set the monument to Joanna Baillie, a poetess and playwright. Her father was the minister at St. Brides when she was born in the manse in 1762, but they left Bothwell when she was only seven. Her father went on to become Professor of Divinity at Glasgow University in 1776, but he died soon after. The family moved to London and Joanna spent the rest of her life in Hampstead, where she is buried. She wrote poetry and plays in verse of which 'Family Legend' was the most successful. Her work was highly praised, especially her poetry in Lowland Scots dialect, and she was a friend of Sir Walter Scott. Her brother Matthew also achieved eminence as the author of the first British treatise on pathology. The monument itself is made of Doulton Ware with four Venetian mosaic panels manufactured by the Murano Glass Company. Facing the street is a portrait of Joanna from a painting by Masquerier. On the eastern side is a portrait of Bothwell Castle with the Clyde at its base, from the famous

The 19th-century spire of Bothwell Parish Church.

painting by Horatio McCulloch. The third panel depicts two young girls supping out of a wooden bowl, while the fourth has apple and plum trees, perhaps to signify the Clyde orchards.

Bothwell retains a charming village atmosphere of bustling shops and winding streets and lanes. From the main street tenements to the grand Victorian villas the buildings have an attractive unity of appearance achieved by the use of local pinky-red sandstone. Many buildings in the main street were originally single storey weavers cottages which have had an extra storey added later. In 1800 there were 92 looms in the village. Most of the larger villas were built in the latter half of the 19th century when transport developments brought Bothwell within easy reach of Glasgow.

The Industrial Revolution however passed Bothwell by, although there was one coal mine in the Castle Policies which opened in 1878. Tenements, now demolished, were built to house the miners on the opposite side of Uddingston Road, under which a passageway was made to take the miners from the colliery to their homes without offending the gaze of the villagers. The tunnel is still there, but the entrances have been blocked up because of its dangerous condition.

Tourism was one industry which was developed in the 19th century. Two railway lines, one Caledonian, one North British, brought holiday makers from the polluted air of Glasgow to the clean air and gentle climate of Bothwell. The present Bothwell Bridge Hotel, originally the Clyde Hotel, was built in the 1870s to accommodate them. The Caledonian station was just across the road on the site of the present Edgecumbe Instruments factory.

Many of the Victorian villas merit closer examination and because of the layout of the village with its narrow lanes and cul de sacs, the best way to do this is on foot. Seven of the listed buildings in Bothwell are private houses. In Old Bothwell Road, the original route from the Bridge to the church, is Woodhead House, built in 1679 and the oldest building intact in the village. At the top of the hill to the right in Orchard Avenue is Anchorage House, built in 1803 for Captain Thomson, Flag Captain to Lord Nelson at the Battle of Trafalgar. In Green Street are two houses designed by 'Greek' Thomson, Greenbank and Gleneden House.

Low Blantyre

To the west of the main road is Blantyre Mill Road which leads to a footbridge high across the River Clyde. Across this bridge, at

The monument to Joanna Baillie, dramatist and poetess, Bothwell.

Low Blantyre is the site of Blantyre Mills, now known primarily for the David Livingstone Memorial Centre. These mills were founded in 1785 by David Dale as a spinning factory and Turkey

Red dye works. Seven years later they were bought by James Monteith of Anderston, but in 1793 commerce was paralysed by the French Revolution and Monteith tried unsuccessfully to persuade Dale to rescind the sale agreement. It was fortunate that Dale refused (he was not that much of a philanthropist) because Monteith made his fortune by converting his unsaleable yarn into highly marketable cloth, selling it at a newly established auction market in London for cotton and linen cloth. On his death in 1802, the business was taken over by his brother, Henry Monteith and it continued to prosper in that family's hands until 1885.

The company had to meet the housing needs of its workers by building a self-contained village beside the mills and it was in one of these tenements that David Livingstone was born. He was employed in the mills from the age of ten but studied hard, even placing books on top of the spinning jennies so that he could read as he worked. That he could absorb any of it, surrounded by the deafening noise of the textile machinery, is amazing. He went on to study medicine at Glasgow University and joined the London Missionary Society immediately after graduating. Once ordained, in 1840, he left to work in Africa, at first in Bechuanaland, then moving north to find trade routes to the east and west, incidentally 'discovering' the Victoria Falls. On his return home in 1856 he severed his connections with the Missionary Society so as to be free to undertake more exploration, and to carry on a campaign against the slave trade. He spent another seventeen years in Africa until his death in 1873. His devoted African servants embalmed his body and carried it hundreds of miles to the coast from where he was shipped home to Britain and buried with honour in Westminster Abbey.

There is little remaining of what was once a large complex of mills and houses. Of buildings, the end two bays of the counting house block and two ranges of housing have been preserved and restored as the David Livingstone Memorial Centre. In the river the curved weir and mill lade can still be seen.

Further along this river bank towards the ruins of Blantyre Priory is a newly reclaimed area, transformed from coal bings into rolling parkland, some of which is destined to become a public golf course. It is a favourite place for walks and affords lovely views of the Clyde and Bothwell Castle. Here are the barely

The David Livingstone Memorial, Low Blantyre.

discernible remains of Blantyre Priory. There are very few historical records relating to the Priory but it is believed that it was dependent on Jedburgh Abbey and was probably established in the reign of and by Alexander II. At the Reformation it ceased to be used as a religious house and became, for a time, the private residence of the Lords of Blantyre. There is a story that Alexander, 4th Lord Blantyre moved to another home in Cardonald, leaving his wife and four children at the Priory. Strange happenings led to the mistress and servants becoming convinced that the house was haunted. Lady Blantyre raised a legal action against her husband, alleging that the house he had given her 'is troubled with an evil spirit and is no ways habitable'. Lord Blantyre had to move back into the Priory while his wife and family moved to the comfort of Cardonald. As Lady Blantyre is also known to have complained that the air in the Priory was 'exceedingly noxious as most rooms are underground', one wonders who was responsible for the supposed haunting.

Bothwell Castle

Directly across the river from the Priory stands Bothwell Castle, even in its present ruinous state an impressive example of medieval Scottish architecture. Because of its political and strategic importance it has been frequently demolished, modified and rebuilt. It was planned by Walter de Moravia who acquired the land in 1242. It subsequently changed hands and shape several times during the Wars of Independence, before being rebuilt by the 3rd Earl of Douglas, Archibald the Grim, who had inherited the castle by marriage. In the 15th century, the castle was forfeited to the Crown by both the Douglases and two subsequent owners, Lord Crichton and Sir John Ramsay, before being returned to the Douglas family in 1488. In the 17th century, the castle, now in a ruinous state was given to the Earl of Forfar who built a new mansion, using the old castle as a quarry. Ironically there was now no trace of this new castle, while the older one still stands.

The castle's site is a rocky peninsula protected on the south and west side by the River Clyde. The original plan of Walter de Moravia was a pentagonal curtain wall with towers at each corner and a massive circular donjon at the western angle. This was 100 feet high and 60 feet in diameter, its walls 15 feet thick, and it was protected by an interior moat and drawbridge. The outside walls were never completed to that plan and subsequent sieges, demolition and pillaging have made it difficult to follow the sequence of construction. It is known that the Douglases completed the walls but around a much smaller area. Both Scots and English managed to hold out against siege attacks for several weeks when they had possession of it, and both sides demolished parts of it rather than leave it useful to the enemy. It is remarkable, therefore, that so much of the castle still stands, and there is bound to be debate as to whether the recent re-building enhances it or not.

Uddingston

The path from Bothwell Castle leads into the village of Uddingston, believed to have been established as a settlement of workers from the Castle. However it later developed as a staging post on the main Glasgow-London coach road, built by Thomas Telford in the 1830s. The Telford bridge over the River Calder survived until recently. The Main Stables were at the back of Wellbank Place and had been converted into dwelling houses in the 19th century, before being demolished in the 20th century.

Bothwell Castle from the air.

Like Bothwell, Uddingston's main occupation in the 18th and early 19th century was weaving. At the start of the Industrial Revolution several small iron works were established, particularly specialising in agricultural implements. Wilkies produced and sold over 10,000 'Improved Ploughs' in the 45 years they operated their foundry in Old Mill Road. But the first large foundry to be tried, failed because the sandy ground on which Uddingston stands, could not bear the weight of heavy machinery, and there were problems with subsidence. The foundry in Crofthead Street was converted into a variety theatre, and Uddingston had to give up its aspirations to large scale industrial expansion.

Later in the 19th century, coal was found in the area and seven mines were opened successfully. The old baths of Viewpark

Tunnock's baker's shop, Main Street, Uddingston.

Colliery still exist having been converted into the outhouses of Viewpark Nursery.

The most successful of Uddingston's businesses celebrated its centenary in 1990 – Tunnock's Bakery. Thomas Tunnock first opened a baker's shop in Bellshill Road, Uddingston in 1890. They moved to Loanhead Mansions, Main Street in 1912 after a fire in the Bellshill Road premises, and the business passed from grandfather to father to son, surviving two World Wars until the introduction of one product turned a local baker into a national institution – Tunnock's Caramel Wafers. It was launched in 1952, when sweets were still rationed, and became an instant best seller. I can remember as a child being taken to the Uddingston tea-rooms where their pet mynah bird, Jacky, declaimed, in a broad Lanarkshire accent 'Tunnocks Caramel Wafers arra best'. The company, still family owned, now supply their products all over the country, and employ over 700 people in Uddingston, making them one of the largest employers in the area.

Like Bothwell, the coming of the railway in the 19th century led to a boom in local house building, and there are several virtually unspoilt Victorian housing developments worth visiting. Douglas Gardens, started in 1868, was the first residential scheme.

It was a D-shaped plan, built around large central gardens. The largest house is St. Peter's Lodge which was built for Doctor Smith, Inspector of Schools for Scotland. He named the house after his Cambridge college rather than the gateway to heaven, but its subsequent owners, the Bishop of Motherwell and then the Holy Ghost Fathers, must have found it very apt. Another of the houses, Monterey, had a wireless station which in 1916 was commandeered for the duration of the war.

The houses at Gardenside Avenue are villas set well back with large gardens sloping down to the street. Number 7 was the first to be built in 1871, and Number 14 which has a specially lovely garden was owned by a Mr. Marshall who collected trees and shrubs. Edina House was owned by a wealthy spirit merchant, Robert Brown, who built Gardenside Terrace on the site of Hamilton's Brickworks to prevent anything detrimental to the value of the Avenue being put there. It is believed that when he installed one of his sons, a drunkard, in Number 5 he had a special railing provided at the front steps.

Kylepark is another small area of Victorian housing down near the river. It takes its name from the maiden name of Mrs. Thomson, wife of the developer. The Crescent is particularly attractive with its terrace houses built on one side of the road only, so that every house has an unrestricted view of the river.

There was very little housebuilding in Uddingston from 1900 until the 1960s when there was an explosion in demand. Fortunately the new developments have not intruded on the old; the unique character of Victorian Uddingston remains intact.

CHAPTER 9

Cambuslang, Rutherglen and Glasgow

After Uddingston, the River Clyde flows into more open
countryside again before reaching the industrial east end of
Glasgow. On the north bank is the small settlement of Carmyle,
established by the Bishops of Glasgow in the 13th century when
they built meal mills here. A local muslin weaving industry
developed in the 1740s and the village grew with the later
discovery of ironstone. In Carmyle Avenue is Carmyle House
designed and built in 1830 by William Burn, the architect best
known for his unsuccessful restoration of St. Giles Cathedral.
Spanning the river is the now disused Carmyle Railway Viaduct,
an elegant lattice steelwork bridge supported by tall tapering
stone piers which carried the Caledonian Railway line to Cambuslang and Hamilton.

Cambuslang

Cambuslang is a conglomeration of several small settlements.
Some like Flemington and Hallside were miners' and weavers'
hamlets, others were country estates, for example Newton and
Morriston. In the 17th century a small village grew around the
parish at Kirkhill where most inhabitants were domestic spinners
and weavers. Coal mining started at the same period and expanded
with the opening of the Clyde Iron Works in 1786. However
Cambuslang did not really have any cohesion as a town until the
late 19th century. Most housing was to accommodate the workers
from the industrial plants which had been set up locally – steel
works, dye-works, heavy engineering – although there was some
middle class housing built further uphill behind Kirkhill Station.
Industrial decline in the 20th century has blighted the area
which is now studded with large derelict tracts of land, while a
dual carriageway has been bulldozed through the main street,
destroying any vestiges of a village atmosphere. Near the river,
one of the few 19th century industrial premises to survive is the
former Rosebank Dyeworks in Somervell Street. Turkey red yarn
was produced here from 1881 until 1945. The building is banded

Romanesque figure of Saint Eloi, patron saint of hammermen.

with a Greek key pattern in white on red brick and has a double pitched roof with a bell turret.

Rutherglen

Adjoining Cambuslang to the west, with a much longer history, is the former Royal Burgh of Rutherglen. It received its Royal Charter in the 12th century and was an important medieval trading centre and port. It was built on a ridge of the Clyde at a point where the river first becomes tidal. It still has a recognizably medieval town plan with wide main street and back wynds. Fragments have been found of an early parish church, including a charming Romanesque statue of St. Eloi, the patron saint of the Incorporation of Hammermen.

Like the previous villages the principal industries in Rutherglen before the 19th century were hand loom weaving and mining. Until 1755 much of the coal produced was sent downstream from Rutherglen quay, despite the river having a maximum depth of only two feet. It was loaded on to flat-bottomed boats called lighters or gabberts which could carry up to three hundred cart-loads of twelve hundredweight each. In summer when the water level fell it was not unknown for these boats to become grounded. Also in the summer months herring boats would bring their cargoes up to Rutherglen to sell.

In 1856 a shipbuilding firm was founded in Rutherglen by Thomas Seath. He leased two acres of land on a bend of the river where he would have space to launch his boats. He specialised in building pleasure steamers, and also operated a summer service on the upper reaches of the Clyde. In his first four month season he carried more than 38,000 passengers but he gave up this side of his business to concentrate on building ships. One of his most famous ships is the *Lucy Ashton* which sailed on the Clyde for sixty years. Seath's also built the first four *Cluthas* which operated a passenger service on the Clyde in the centre of Glasgow until the electric trams and the Underground took all their passengers.

Gradually the quayside in Rutherglen was completely taken over by industrial premises, just as the cottages in the town were replaced by tenement accommodation for their workers. After the Second World War, when these industries had died, the 19th century developments were themselves cleared away, in some places replaced by housing schemes, in others left derelict.

The Winter Garden, Glasgow Green.

Glasgow

The Clyde winds on into the east end of Glasgow, passing by Richmond Park where mock naval battles are fought out on Sundays by the model boat enthusiasts. Fathers perform tricky manoeuvres, radar sensors turning, guns firing while their sons look on enviously wishing they were allowed to play. The river then passes under the St. Andrews Footbridge, built in 1853-55 in wrought iron, with cast iron pylons shaped like fluted Corinthian columns. It was built to enable workers from both sides of the river to move easily between the areas of Hutchesontown and Bridgeton and Calton, which shared their workforces in similar industries of textiles and engineering.

On the north bank of the river is Glasgow Green, a site of great historical importance to the City, although the City fathers have not always thought so. It has served many and varied purposes over the years. From medieval times it was used as common grazing land, right up until the end of the 19th century, by which time the authorities were charging a fixed price for each animal and employing a herdsman to supervise the grazing. It continued to be used as a washing and bleaching green by the local community despite attempts to turn it into a 'park' with carriageways and shrubberies in the 19th century. Many large political and religious meetings have been held here and the area of the Green between Nelson's Monument and the Courthouse was Glasgow's equivalent of Hyde Park Corner, where anyone was entitled to air their views – until the Corporation passed a bye-law against it, that is, in 1916.

Some of Glasgow's oldest sporting clubs started on the Green. The Glasgow Golf Club was formed in 1787, although we know golf was played before that. James Watt mentions the Golf-house in his account of his famous walk on the Green during which he conceived the idea for a separate condenser. There is now a monument to him beside Nelson's Monument, raised on the bicentenary of his invention in 1965. In the 19th century both Rangers and Celtic Football Clubs started here and in 1899 Fleshers Haugh at the extreme east end of the Green was laid out as public playing fields.

There have been many threats to the Green's survival – by the 16th century most of it had been sold off and the City had to buy parcels of land to extend it again. In the period at the turn of the 18th century sections were again sold off to developers. In the 19th century there were proposals to build a railway viaduct across it and a coal mine under it – both of which were fiercely resisted by the people of Glasgow who had come to regard it as their place. The same reaction was provoked more recently by plans to build a motorway across it.

Set in the park is the People's Palace, built in the 1890s for the recreation and improvement of the people of the East End. It had reading rooms on the ground floor, a museum on the first floor and picture galleries at the top. Since 1940 it has housed Glasgow's local history collection. At the rear of the building is the massive Winter Garden four times the size of the Museum, supposedly shaped in the form of the hull of Nelson's flag ship, Victory. This has been recently restored and is used as an atmospheric concert venue.

Beside St. Andrews Bridge is a house occupied by the Glasgow Humane Society Officer. In 1787 James Coulter, a Glasgow merchant, left £200 in the care of the Faculty of Surgeons to set up a society for the rescue and recovery of drowning persons and in 1790 the Glasgow Humane Society was formed. It is now the only one of its kind left in existence. A boathouse and house were built on the Green in 1796, but there was no full-time officer appointed until George Geddes in 1859. The longest serving officer was the dedicated Ben Parsonage who devoted his life to his job, saving over 300 lives in his 51 years of service.

Behind the Green is an extraordinarily extrovert piece of architecture for these northern climes. The Moorish-Italianate design of Templeton's Carpet Factory, now known as the Templeton Business Centre, was based on the Doge's Palace, Venice to advertise that exotic carpets were being manufactured inside. One of Templeton's earliest carpets was exhibited at the Crystal Palace International Exhibition in 1851, when it was stood on by no less a personage than Queen Victoria herself. It had been designed for the Royal Reception Room, after which it was in use in the British Embassy in Washington for 78 years before being returned for repair. After restoration it was gifted to the Smithsonian Museum where it is now displayed.

To the west of the Green lies the site of the oldest part of the city of Glasgow. There has been so much rebuilding here that it is impossible to see any remnants of the 18th century layout. The area lies between Buchanan Street and High Street and between Ingram Street and the Clyde. Originally residential, the buildings quickly changed to warehousing when trade prospered and the wealthy moved their homes to the more fashionable west end of town. In the last twenty years this area has been revitalised and re-christened the Merchant City. Old warehouses have been converted into city flats and new shops and restaurants have opened. Many of Glasgow's markets were situated here: the City market in Candleriggs, the cheese market in Walls Street, the fish market at the Briggait in Clyde Street. Attempts to turn these into shopping malls have not been a financial success.

The street along the riverside, Clyde Street, was previously rather a hotch-potch of residential and industrial premises. The town's slaughterhouses were at the east end and there was ware-housing along the quays, yet three mansions were built here. One of them, the Dreghorn Mansion, survived until recently although swallowed up inside a carpet warehouse. Photographs taken of it before its demolition show the beautiful plasterwork which decorated the interior.

Further along is the Briggait, the former fish market. It was built in the 1870s in a French classical style. It has an elaborate frontage with two columned gateways and cast ironwork decoration. The former Merchants' House stood on this site and its steeple remains, emerging out of the roof of the Fish Market. It is 17th century, Gothic in style and topped with a golden ship on a globe, the emblem of the Merchants House.

Also on Clyde Street is Glasgow's Roman Catholic Cathedral of St. Andrews by James Gillespie, built in 1814–17. This beautiful late Perpendicular style church is not seen to advantage now, being hemmed in on one side by its own modern yellow brick house and overshadowed from behind by Glasgow's giant greenhouse, the St. Enoch Centre, winner of a Saltire Award.

The next section of river bank to the west is called the Broomielaw and it was the first terminal for trading ships. Beside it is the headquarters of the Clyde Navigation Trust, now renamed the Clyde Port Authority. The older part of the building was designed by J.J. Burnet and constructed in the 1880s, while the extravagant corner section was added some twenty years later. Architecturally the building is rather unbalanced by this extension but recent cleaning has revealed wonderful sculpture and carving which more than compensate. Their subject matter ranges from ancient mythology to the everyday world of the Clyde and the City: there are figures of both Europa and her bull and of Henry Bell and the *Comet;* the ship emblem of the Trust is flanked by naked putti. Up until the 18th century Glasgow had not been too concerned by its lack of city centre harbour facilities but the establishment of colonies in America changed that. In all other respects it was in an ideal position to become a major trading centre. The first solution was to find deep water facilities further downstream and after being refused land in Dumbarton, they managed to acquire a site beside Newark Castle which they named, imaginatively, Port Glasgow. Their first Custom House opened there in 1710. In the next fifty years the Town Council made no attempt to deepen the channel upstream from Port Glasgow: in fact the inhabitants were doing their best to choke it up completely by dumping all their sewage and rubbish into it. This resulted in an even lower water level and frequent flooding. In 1722 work was started on a new quay at Broomielaw which had been unchanged for sixty years and this work was completed in 1726. The tobacco trade was of paramount importance to the City and the Tobacco Lords began to campaign to have the Clyde deepened.

52 Charlotte Street, the only surviving Georgian mansion in Calton, restored by the National Trust.

In 1768 John Golborne visited Glasgow to discuss the building of a cross-country canal, but was also consulted about the problem of deepening the Clyde. He reported that because the sides of the river were of a much softer material than the bottom, the river current was eroding the banks and leaving the river bed intact. His suggested solution was to narrow the channel by building projecting dykes in pairs from both the north and south banks thus increasing the speed of the current which in turn would increase the erosion of the river bed. Dredging would also be necessary to help shift the sandbanks, such as Dumbuck, which formed major obstructions. Work started in 1771 after an Act of Parliament had been obtained making Glasgow Town Council Trustees of the Clyde Navigation. The overall success of Golborne's operations delighted the people of Glasgow for within two years there was a minimum depth of five feet at high tide throughout the length of the river. This depth was gradually increased enabling the sea-going traders to bring their goods directly into the city centre. The quay at Broomielaw was extended west to York Street and residential development was replaced by more warehousing accommodation, used initially for tea then later as bonded warehousing for tobacco and whisky. At 34 Robertson Lane, a warehouse built in 1800 still survives but most of the other warehousing there today is from a later period, the best examples being in James Watt Street. Thirty years ago there was a terrible fire in one of these whisky bonds in Cheapside Street when many firemen lost their lives.

Westward from the Broomielaw along the river front is Lancefield Quay where the old cargo sheds have recently been transformed into elegant flats commanding a lovely riverside view and a very high price. Towering over them is the largest of the Glasgow bridges, the Kingston Bridge. It has a clearance height of 60 feet to allow dredgers to pass underneath and is 138 feet wide. Between here and Yorkhill was the village of Finnieston which was swallowed up in the industrial expansion of the 19th century which in turn has been obliterated by 20th century redevelopment.

On Finnieston Quay stands a massive crane, now one of the riverside's best known landmarks, erected in 1931 for the Clyde Navigation Trust. The 175 ton cantilever crane was intended specifically for loading Glasgow built locomotives on to ships for export. Beside it is the North Rotunda of the Finnieston harbour tunnel. Opened in 1896, there were three parallel tunnels, one for pedestrians and two for horse-drawn traffic. Each rotunda had stairs for the pedestrians and for the vehicles, six hydraulic lifts. Since the tunnels were closed in 1986 the North Rotunda has been converted into a restaurant complex, while the South Rotunda was a cafeteria during the Glasgow Garden Festival and is now closed. Also situated on Finnieston Quay is the Scottish Exhibition Centre, a characterless building reminiscent of an aircraft hangar surrounded by large expanses of tarmacadam carparks. At the western end of the quay is the dock's former hydraulic pumping station – an attractive Italianate building which has been stone-cleaned and converted into three restaurants, the fish restaurant in a glass extension at the back taking full advantage of its riverside views.

Across the river Kelvin are Meadowside Granaries built by the Clyde Navigation Trust in 1911-13. The Trustees had bought Meadowside in 1907 to complete their line of berthage west of the Kelvin. The only occupant of the land was Partick Thistle Football Club who agreed to relocate to a ground in Maryhill. Imports of grain to the Clyde had grown in proportion to the increase in the population of Glasgow and shipowners had been

Glasgow and Strathkelvin Sheriff Court.

complaining about the lack of facilities to unload their grain cargoes quickly. In response to this the Trust built this large granary at Meadowside, equipped with the most up-to-date equipment available; the grain was unloaded by conveyor belts each fitted with 166 small buckets in a system similar to that of a bucket dredger. Their first cargo was unloaded from the Hornby on May 14, 1914. Just beyond the granaries is the entrance to the new Clyde Tunnel which was planned just after the Second World War when there was still enough shipping coming into the city to make a bridge impractical.

Occupying the south bank of the Clyde from St. Andrews Bridge to the Mavisbank Quay is the Gorbals. It was a village surrounded by farmland when it was bought up by Trade and Merchant Houses and the Town Council who hoped to find coal there. However coal mining ventures were never financially successful and with escalating land values in the late 18th century, Gorbals was sold off to property developers. James Laurie, a surveyor, drew up ambitious plans for a new town where there was to be uniformity in the width of the streets and the style and height of the houses. These plans were unfortunately overtaken by the expansion in trade and industry. The local people were crammed into overcrowded housing until the City Development Trust made clearances of the worst slums between 1871 and 1891. The population statistics speak for their success: in 1871 the population was 44,042 and by 1891 it had been reduced to 39,806. However, after the Depression and the Second World War, the name of the Gorbals had become synonymous with poverty and deprivation, causing the planners of the 1950s to choose wholesale clearance as their best course of action. As often happens the good went with the bad, leaving individual public buildings like the library standing alone in the middle of patches of wasteground. Fortunately this policy changed before Laurieston was reached and the beautiful buildings of Carlton Place have been preserved.

Along Adelphi Street the buildings of interest are more recent. The School of Nautical Studies used to specialise in teaching the skills required to sail ships but now that Glasgow's importance as a port has declined, the College teaches more general subjects too. The building is meant to resemble a ship with its white exterior topped by radar masts and the deck area towards the jetty. Like a ship, women were considered unlucky to have aboard and female staff, until recently, were confined to the annexe.

Occupying another riverside site is the Glasgow Central Mosque which was completed in 1984. This adds an oriental feature to the Glasgow skyline with its multi-faceted golden dome and slender minaret. Across from it in Gorbals Street is the new Glasgow and Strathkelvin Sheriff Court. Built of beautiful stone and facing the river, it still has a rather grim and imposing appearance, perhaps well suited to its function.

At the river beyond King George V bridge are two quays built by the Clyde Navigation Trust in the early stages of their dockside expansion. Clyde Place Quay, opposite the Broomielaw, was built by Charles Atherton, the first engineer to be employed by them, and it was first used in 1837. The site for Windmillcroft Quay was purchased in 1839, the original proposal being to create a dock with a surface area of fifteen acres, accommodating 150 ships, but this idea was dropped and linear quayage was constructed instead, adding another 335 yards to quays to the riverbank.

Beside the Kingston Bridge the Co-operative Wholesale Society's headquarters are an impressive complex of warehouses and offices although they look as if they should have a much grander function. In a flamboyant mixture of Flemish, French

The North Rotunda, Finnieston.

and Jacobean styles, they are an impressive advertisement for the success of the Co-operative Movement. In this area the motorway has cut a swathe through the townscape, giving a clear view of one of Rennie Mackintosh's public buildings, Scotland Street School. Much plainer than the School of Art, it conforms to the School Board's prerequisites, while incorporating his own individual style. The large areas of glass in relation to stonework is immediately striking, especially in the two stair towers pulled out at either end of the front of the school. A touch of Scottish Baronial is added by the pointed caps topping these towers. This building is now a Museum of Education where local children can experience for themselves just what Victorian schooldays were like.

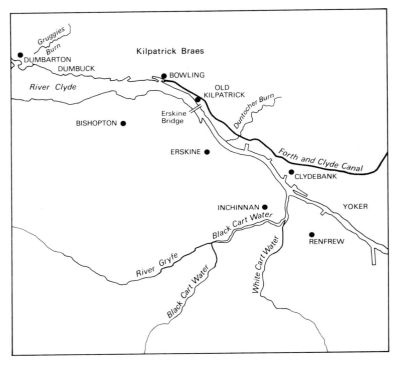

Renfrew to Dumbarton.

CHAPTER 10

Govan, Renfrew, Yoker and Clydebank

Govan

The parish of Govan, as erected in 1771, was in two equal parts north and south of the river, a situation which was, according to the minister in 1790, extremely inconvenient. There was no bridge, the quay on the north bank had been sanded up since the deepening operations and the ferry was privately owned and neglected. The main occupations on the south bank were farming, salmon fishing and weaving. The houses were old and insanitary and there was no local baker, butcher or public market – not an attractive place to live. The industry which transformed this village was ship-building.

The first yard to open in Govan was Mackie and Thomson's in 1840, but the most influential was Robert Napier's which opened in 1841. Napier was primarily a marine engineer and at first sub-contracted the building of the hulls to other yards before moving in to the premises in Govan East Yard, where he could build for himself. He was associated with the Dennys and with David Elder and so many of the shipbuilders of the Clyde received their training in his employ that he was later to be known as the 'Father of Clyde Shipbuilding'.

David Elder, who had started with Robert Napier, became a partner in his own marine engineering firm, Randolph Elder & Company, in 1852. The innovative steam compound engine they designed for the coastal steamer *SS Brandon* guaranteed their success and they were soon looking for new premises. In 1864 he laid out a new yard in Govan which started operating four years later. Unfortunately, Elder died in 1869, aged only forty five, but under the direction of William Pearce the yard went on to build some of the most technically advanced ships produced on the Clyde. Many of their liners were holders of the Blue Riband for the fastest crossings of the Atlantic. They also built the strange turbot-shaped yacht *Livadia* for the Russian Royal Family. It was designed for safety, the previous Royal Yacht having sunk in the Black Sea. The *Livadia* was 235 feet long and 153 feet wide: a

133

model of it is on display in the Transport Museum in the Kelvin Hall.

Sadly the Czar died a year after its launch and the *Livadia* ended its days as a coal transporter. In 1885 Elders changed its name to Fairfield Shipbuilding and Engineering Company and survived as such until 1935 when it was bought by Lithgows. Temporarily absorbed by Upper Clyde Shipbuilders in 1968 it managed to regain independence as Govan Shipbuilders. The yard is now owned by a Norwegian firm, Kvaerner, which has been building large container ships and highly specialised liquid petroleum gas carriers.

Another important yard in Govan which disappeared into UCS was Stephen and Sons which opened in Linthouse in 1868 having moved from an earlier site in Kelvinhaugh. Like Elders it established its own engine works but specialised in a rather different kind of boat, concentrating on cargo-passenger vessels, particularly elegant banana boats for the West Indian trade.

To illustrate just what a difference the shipbuilding industry made to Govan, one has only to compare the size of the population in 1864 when John Elder first bought his site and 1904 when marine engineering was flourishing. In 1864 there were only 9,000 people living in Govan, by 1904 there were almost 91,000. The two burgh halls built at either end of this forty year period are still standing and are an interesting contrast to each other: the earlier is a dimple design by J. Burnet and is now the police station in Orkney Street, while the later, in Govan Road, is a much grander design in red sandstone decorated with elaborate carvings. The burgh, which was not annexed by Glasgow until 1912, received a great deal of help from the shipyard owners in the provision of local amenities: Lady Pearce gave the Working Men's Institute which is still very much a hub of the community today. Lady Elder, widow of John Elder, was particularly generous, providing a park, a library, a hospital and an infirmary. She also financed a Chair of Naval Architecture at Glasgow University.

During this period of great prosperity, it was decided to replace the barely fifty year old parish church with a new building. So while the site of Govan Parish Church is very old, the present church was completed only in 1888. Designed by Rowand Anderson, it now stands in a prominent position on the riverbank when only forty years ago it was surrounded by shipyards. Inside

Traction engine at the Clyde Foundry, Govan.

the church are kept some remarkable examples of early Christian sculptures. Particularly fine are the hog-backed stones thought to date from the 10th century, the lids carved to resemble roof tiles, the sides covered with animal carvings. There is also an 11th century sarcophagus decorated with interlacing patterns and hunting scenes. This has been made from one huge block of sandstone, laboriously hollowed out to serve as a coffin.

In the 1880s the Navigation Trust decided to build Glasgow's third dock complex to the east of Govan Cross on the Cessnock Estate. To avoid paying inflated land prices, individual Trustees bought the land in small parcels, then, when the whole site was acquired, resold it to the Trust as cost price. Although the quays were opened gradually as each was completed, the whole complex was not officially opened and named until 1897. Princes Dock was intended to cater for the cargo trade, and because it had been fitted out with the best facilities, berthage was quickly taken up by major shipowners. Because of the decline in trade after the Second World War, Princes Dock was closed down in the 1970s. Part of its site was infilled when it was used very successfully for the Glasgow Garden Festival in 1988, prior to it being used for housing development.

The two miles of river frontage from Stephen's Yard at Linthouse to the Renfrew Ferry were bought by the Trustees in 1905. They had an ambitious plan, put forward by their engineer William Alston, to create five parallel tidal basins, giving 8200 yards of quays. Construction was delayed by the Great War but approval was given to start on the first easternmost basin in 1923. It was a period of recession and high unemployment so external pressure was brought to bear for the work to go ahead, thus providing employment for up to 1500 men. The Government gave financial aid to encourage the scheme. George V Dock opened in 1931 and although initially underused, it proved invaluable during the Second World War, handling supplies from the United States, including airplanes transferring from ship to Renfrew Airport. Even now George V Dock is still busy, providing the main non-containerised general cargo-berths on the Clyde. These cargoes consist mainly of steel, machinery and whisky.

Renfrew

The town of Renfrew is set back from the river, and although the county town and a burgh since the 1150s, it has always been overshadowed by its more prosperous neighbour Paisley. However Renfrew does have the distinction of being one of the most ancient crossing points on the Clyde. In medieval times the shallowness of the river at Marlin Ford allowed crossing by foot at low tide, while at high tide a raft was used. By 1614 the right of ferry was included in the charter given to the town by King James VI. The ferry was later moved downstream from its original site by Alexander Speirs, a tobacco merchant who had built himself a mansion at Kings Inch close by the access road to the ferry. Wishing more privacy, Speirs asked that the ferry be moved half a mile downstream closer to Renfrew and offered in return to build two new quays, a ferry house, stables and a new access road. The council were delighted to accept and offered to contribute to the cost of a new ferry boat which would increase the number of passengers and therefore their revenue. The industrial expansion in the area after 1850 had resulted in greater traffic of workers moving from one side of the Clyde to the other, and in 1868 the steam powered ferry was put into service. The diesel electric chain ferry which served as an arts venue during Glasgow's

Engine of the steam tug, the Clyde, memorial to Andrew Brown

year as European City of Culture was introduced in 1952. The industrial decline in the 1960s reduced the number of passengers again and in 1984 the vehicular ferry was replaced by a small motor launch which transports pedestrians across on a request basis – coming more or less full circle to its beginnings.

The Navigation Trust went to great lengths to prevent Renfrew Town Council with some partners developing the quayside at Renfrew for themselves. The Trustees believed that they should have exclusive rights to control all quayage and docks on the Clyde and had already successfully blocked other proposed developments by private concerns. However the Trust were destined to become the principal customer of the shipbuilders who were based on the Renfrew shoreline. William Simons and Company were founded in Greenock in 1810 but opened a yard in Renfrew in the 1860s run by William Simons junior and Andrew Brown, a marine engineer who was to become renowned as a designer of dredging equipment. The Trustees placed their first order with them for the two self-propelled hopper barges for which Andrew Brown created an entirely new design which meant that the dredgings could be disposed of very quickly and easily – at that time at the mouth of Loch Long. The yard then specialised in the dredging plant which was so vital to the Trust in their constant battle to prevent the channel of the Clyde from silting up. When the Trust needed new repair yards for their dredging fleet the obvious choice was a site at Renfrew beside these yards, and in 1908 they had completed the necessary wharves, machine shops and slipway. On the shore nearby is an unusual memorial to Andrew Brown – his engines from the paddle tug, the Clyde, taken out of service in 1912, erected on the town's Low Green as a tribute to him.

Just before the bridge over the White Cart is a small monument to the Earl of Argyll who in 1685 tried to lead an army of 2,000 men in an attack on Glasgow. When they were stopped at Old Kilpatrick, the Earl tried to escape capture by crossing the river but was caught at Renfrew. He was taken to Edinburgh where he was later beheaded for treason. Two small unmarked stones said to come from a cross marking a shrine of St. Conval are his only memorial.

Across the river Cart is the parish of Inchinnan which is more associated with the development of aviation than ships. The engineering firm, Beardmore, was involved with pioneering aeroplane design in their factory at Dalmuir and these were test-flown from the airstrip at Inchinnan, later to become Renfrew Airport. Of their first five prototype aircraft, designed by Lieutenant G.T. Richards, only the third was at all successful and several hundred of this bomber were produced during the Great War. By the end of the War, Beardmore had manufactured approximately 650 aeroplanes. However Beardmore used their Inchinnan site for the building of a much larger form of air transport – the airship. When A.J. Balfour took over from Winston Churchill as First Lord of the Admiralty in 1915, he investigated the usefulness of airships in a war situation. He was impressed by the use the Germans made of them as spy planes during sea battles. Several firms were asked to submit designs and quotations and Beardmore received orders for 23-class airships. With guarantees of more orders to come an enormous shed was built at Inchinnan, with funding from the Government, in which to construct the airships. There were considerable pro-duction problems and the airships proved extremely difficult to manoeuvre on the ground. A Government order for three airships placed in January 1917 was not completed before the end of the war. With peace came an interest in the civilian trans-

Beardmore's airship construction shed at Inchinnan, 1918.

port potential of the airship and an R34 built at Inchinnan made a test flight from Edinburgh to the USA. However it took 108 hours, only a few hours less than a ship, and commercial civilian flights were never a possibility. Beardmore Aero Engines Ltd. were put into liquidation in 1921.

Yoker

The north bank of this same stretch of river also developed a thriving shipbuilding industry. In Yoker, they owed their prosperity to the encouragement they gave to an enterprising, gifted English marine engineer called Alfred Yarrow to bring his business north from London. He had started business in Poplar on the Isle of Dogs. An unusual boat-building technique which was to become his speciality was started quite by chance. Funds raised in memory of David Livingstone were to be spent on providing a river launch to sail on Lake Nyasa in the campaign against the slave trade. Yarrow was approached to see if he could build a launch which could then be taken to pieces of no more than 50lbs weight each and reassembled by unskilled labour at Lake Nyasa. Interested by this challenge, he solved the problem by having plates which were bolted together not riveted, and he made the boilers in circular sections so that could be rolled across the ground. His method proved so successful that he opened up an enormous market around the world for pre-fabricated river and lake launches. One of the largest ships to be assembled overseas this way was the *RMS Victoria* for passenger service on Lake Victoria. She could carry 730 passengers and was 260 feet long, yet she was sent out of Africa in small pieces, all numbered, port side painted red, starboard green and rebuilt by local workers supervised by only three of Yarrow's staff. This was not a 19th century project as one might imagine – she was launched in 1960.

Yarrows has also been most closely associated with the development of the torpedo boat and the destroyer. After self-propelled torpedoes were invented in 1877, Yarrow built a sample boat to carry them for the Admiralty. His design was a success and governments from other countries were quick to order this new type of naval vessel from him. By 1900 he had established his reputation as a builder of innovation and excellence and his business had expanded greatly. He started looking for a new site for his yard with a view to cutting his costs. Since the change from wood to iron as the main building material, the shipbuilding industry on the Thames was doomed. It was too far for the supply of raw materials and transport costs meant that pricing could not be competitive with the shipyards in the north. Yarrow was courted in the same manner we accord to potential Japanese manufacturers today, and he chose the Clydeside site at Yoker as sounding the most welcoming. With typical speed and efficiency he began moving plant north immediately after signing the feu agreement. In July 1908 his first destroyer was launched on the Clyde. He brought 300 of his workforce with him, even building brick English style cottages for them when they did not like the Scottish tenements. Although the locals did not believe they would last more than five years they are still standing today in Riversdale, Thomden and Ardsley Lanes. Yarrows have most recently been involved in the building of new Type 23 frigates for the Royal Navy. All are named after dukes, the most recent being *HMS Iron Duke* launched in March 1991.

Clydebank

Further downstream on the north bank is the town of Clydebank which was named after its shipyard. Two brothers, James and George Thomson set up and engine and boiler works in Finnieston in 1847, but with a steadily expanding market they were able to

The launch of the *Kyoto Forest* on 7th November 1969 at Upper Clyde Shipbuilders, Clydebank, arranged by launch manager, John M. Cowan, foreground.

move to larger premises at Govan, renaming their business the Clyde Bank Shipyard. During the twenty one years they were based there, they built over one hundred ships, including the *Iona* which was sunk off Gourock after having been sold to the Confederate States for blockade-running during the American Civil War. The Thomsons had to move their Govan site when the Trust built Princes Dock, to a new position at West Barns, Kilbowie, where they not only had a large land area on which to develop their yard, they were also directly opposite the mouth of the river Cart. This meant that they had room to build and launch even the largest of vessels. At first there was no accommodation for their workforce and they had to be ferried to work from Glasgow daily, but new housing was quickly built. When the new town came to be named the choice was between Kilbowie and Clydebank. Common usage had established the name of the shipyard as the name of the place, so Clydebank it officially became.

After the company became incorporated in 1890, the

controlling share was held by John Browns of Sheffield who specialised in the manufacture of armour plating. Buying controlling interests in shipyards assured them of a market for their product. Control did ultimately pass to others but the name of John Brown has endured. They have built some of the largest merchant and warships to sail out of the Clyde, including the largest of all, the *Queen Mary,* which was almost abandoned before completion. Hull 534 was a victim of the economic depression of the 1930s and lay untouched for over two years before the Government offered Cunard a deal – a repayable loan to finish the *Queen Mary* on condition Cunard took over the ailing White Star Line. It took four hundred men a month to remove one hundred and thirty tons of rust. Work resumed on the 26th May 1934 and the *Queen Mary* was launched on the 26th September of the same year. In the 1960s after the launch of the last of the great liners, the *Queen Elizabeth II,* the yard had to search for new markets. It was the age of oil exploration and the company began to build oil rigs. They were bought over by a Texas company, Marathon who, eight years later in 1980 sold it to UIE, a French company who are still building rigs there today.

The importance of shipbuilding in the area made Clydebank a victim of wartime bombing. On two consecutive nights in March 1941 the Luftwaffe carried out intensive bombing attacks on Clydeside, trying to destroy not only the shipyards but also the heavy engineering factories and oil depots. Incendiary bombs were dropped first to give the pilots some light. With these they managed to hit Yoker Distillery and Singer's timber yard. Many parachute bombs were also dropped, causing a lot of damage to property. In Clydebank only eight of the twelve thousand houses were undamaged and four hundred and ninety six people were killed. There was a great deal of local anger when the press reported light bombing and minimal casualties, which even allowing for wartime restrictions on damage reports was felt to be extremely callous. One witness who was among a group who had taken shelter in the crypt of a church when the incendiaries started falling, describes hearing torrential rain and deciding to stay in the crypt until morning. When they emerged, the church had been completely gutted by fire and they would certainly have died if they had tried to leave their shelter.

The noise they had heard had been the roaring of the flames.

The *Yoker Swan.*

Surprisingly, the Luftwaffe managed to do very little damage to John Brown's or any of the other works on the river.

Rothesay Dock at Clydebank, now deserted, was built by the Clyde Navigation Trust primarily as a coal and mineral dock, for which they provided the most advanced equipment. They had decided that electricity was the best way to power the coal hoists but had to go to Germany to buy them. It was also necessary to build their own power station to supply the large amount of electricity they required. This dock when completed in 1911 could handle at least sixteen ore-carrying steamers at once and the speedy and efficient service ensured that the dock was a commercial success.

Clydebank was also famous for its sewing machine factory – Singers. This American company first opened a sales office in Glasgow in 1856. Ten years later, their marketing had been so successful that they felt able to open a small assembly plant, the components being imported from the USA. Demand continued to outstrip capacity, even after a larger self-sufficient factory had opened in Bridgeton. The parent company decided that all the operations should be brought together on one large site at Kilbowie, conveniently near to the railway, road and canal links.

The Singer clock tower, demolished 1961.

It was a massive complex – machine shops, forge, gasworks, boiler shops – the main buildings were eight hundred feet long and the huge clock tower became a local landmark. At its peak in 1913, Singer was employing fourteen thousand people and producing twentyfive thousand sewing machines a week. Because almost half the output was exported to Russia, Singer decided to open a factory there. There was never a more classic example of bad timing – it was no sooner completed than it was confiscated by the Revolutionary Government and the company never really recovered from that heavy loss. It suffered badly during the Depression, the workforce dropping to four hundred and twenty two in 1932. During the Second World War, its production capacity was devoted to the war effort: bullets and bayonets were made in the foundry and the production of industrial sewing machines was increased. After a short-lived post-was boom, the firm foundered under the onslaught of cheap competition, firstly from Europe, then from Japan. Singers had never invested in modernisation: even some machine tools bought for the opening of the first factory in 1867 were still in use in the 1960s. In 1961 rationalisation was attempted. The old buildings and the famous clock were demolished and a new single storey factory replaced it. As a sign of the company's confidence in the UK market, they invested in the most advanced equipment and streamlined lower and middle management. In 1975, despite the fact that the firm had not made any profits since the 1960s, Singer announced that they were creating another five hundred jobs at Clydebank while closing another factory at Blankenloch in Germany. However in 1979 Singer decided to close down Clydebank which had the lowest productivity of all their European factories and could be shut without disrupting production elsewhere. There was a long hard fight by the trade unions and the workers to save their jobs but the factory shut for the last time in June 1980.

Despite the passing of its heavy industries Clydebank is once again a thriving town. New small industries have been encouraged to open premises here and it is the home of Radio Clyde, one of the most successful commercial radio stations. The town has become a service centre with a large shopping precinct and a wide selection of entertainment including a cinema, a bowling alley and, of course, the 'Bankies', the local football team, who have a loyal following.

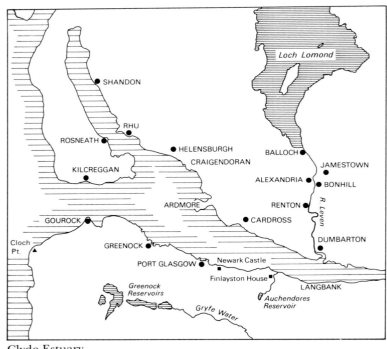

Clyde Estuary.

CHAPTER 11

Old Kilpatrick to Helensburgh

Old Kilpatrick and Bowling

The road, railway and canal run in a parallel course between the Clyde and the Old Kilpatrick Hills through the villages of Old Kilpatrick and Bowling. This was the north-western tip of the Roman Empire, and though no visible traces remain, the Antonine Wall ended here at a large fort, which was excavated in 1923-4 before the Gavinburn site was destroyed by housing development. The fort covered an area of four acres and predates the Wall itself. The administrative block and granary were of stone, while the soldiers' barracks were timber-framed. Some coins and broken pottery were found on the site and are now in the Hunterian museum at Glasgow University.

Because Old Kilpatrick is the legendary birthplace of St Patrick, the site of the parish church is very old. Its lands belonged to Paisley Abbey until the Reformation, when most of it was acquired by the Hamiltons of Barns and Cochno. The present church was built in 1812.

The dominant features of the shoreline are the oil storage tanks. These depots were built at the end of the First World War during which oil had become a very important commodity. Space, safety factors and river depth made this out-of-town site an ideal choice for oil storage. The Admiralty built its depot first in 1918 primarily to supply naval vessels with bunker fuel. A similar facility was built at Bowling by the Clyde Navigation Trust shortly afterwards. This site is now an Esso Oil Terminal where tankers from Grangemouth unload their cargoes of refined products for subsequent distribution to the West of Scotland. Within this terminal is Dunglass Castle and an obelisk monument to Henry Bell, the steamship pioneer. This castle was built for the Colquhoun family, anciently known as de Kilpatrick, and was the residence of John Colquhoun, Chamberlain of Scotland from 1439 to 1478. The Castle suffered several assaults and the last attacks on it by the Covenanters in the 17th century left it a ruin. In the 19th century a new house was built within its walls which

Bowling Harbour, 1991

became a meeting place for artists of the Glasgow Art Nouveau style when it was occupied in the 1890s by Talwin Morris, art director of the publisher William Blackie. Charles Rennie Mackintosh owed him his commission to build Hill House in Helensburgh for Blackie. Mackintosh designed the interior of Dunglass House when it was bought by his father-in-law, Mr Macdonald. The house is now empty and closed up and its contents dispersed among collections both public and private. The Castle may be visited by the public – just ask at the terminal gatehouse and you will be shown around.

In the 18th century Bowling had a small printworks which later became a distillery, but it really grew with the opening of the Forth and Clyde Canal in 1790. With its constant depth of seven feet, the Canal proved a more popular route to the city than the river. In the late 18th century, the port at Stockingfield was much busier than the Broomielaw. According to Custom House records of 1780, the *Triton* arrived in the Broomielaw from Dublin with a cargo of brandy. There is then a three month gap before the next ship, the *Peggy* from the Isle of Man. In the same period, twenty ships a week were coming in through the Canal. Bowling has two large basins connected by locks which have been kept in working order, and the harbourmaster's house is still there. It is an interesting place to explore on foot or bicycle on the recently opened cycle path which runs from Glasgow to Loch Lomond. Details of its route can be obtained from Tourist Information Centres.

Dumbarton and the Vale of Leven

Standing at the mouth of the River Leven, guarding the town of Dumbarton, is Dumbarton Rock, a volcanic plug with two peaks. It is reputed to have the longest recorded history of any fortification in Britain. It was the principal stronghold of the Britons of Strathclyde when it was known by the Gaels as Dunbreatann – rock of the Britons – now corrupted to Dumbarton. Alexander II acquired the Castle for use as a royal fortress in the 13th century, and in the 16th century, Thomas Crawford of Gartnavel captured it from Queen Mary's forces. It has frequently been used as a prison. It held William Wallace in 1305, the Pretender's supporters after the 1745 Rebellion and at the turn of that century soldiers from Napoleon's armies. Most of the buildings on the Rock now date from the 18th century when there was a major reconstruction and the Governor's House was built. During the Second World War the Rock was equipped with anti-aircraft guns to counter the German attacks on the ships and yards of the Clyde. Just to the east of the Rock is Gruggie's Burn where Blackburns launched their Sunderland Flying Boats during the war.

The town of Dumbarton sits on an alluvial plain, and used to be frequently flooded by both the Leven and the Clyde. The centre is a small area on the bend of the Leven, now unfortunately completely dominated by an enormous whisky distillery, quite out of proportion to the buildings around it. The most important local industries prior to shipbuilding were glass-making and chemicals. The chemical industry was an off-shoot from the textile factories in the Vale of Leven, and was mostly involved in the dyeing process, being especially famous for its 'turkey red' dye. The cones of Dixon's glass works used to tower over the town as the distillery does now. Founded in 1777, it produced fine bottle and window glass, but went out of business in the 1850s when cheap glass was imported from Austria.

The glassworks site was taken over by Peter Denny and John Tulloch for their marine engineering works in 1851. The dynasty of Denny shipbuilders began with William Denny, who in 1814 had built the *Margery*, the first steamer to operate on the Thames. His sons formed the firm of William Denny and Bros. which survived until the 1960s when it was crippled by the development costs of a prototype hovercraft. The company was always in the forefront of technical and scientific development, and was unique in Britain in having the only privately-owned experiment tank. William Denny II had been intrigued by William Froude's work at the Admiralty Tank in Torquay, and in 1875, had sent him plans of a ship he was building to be tested. The results were so impressive that he made one of the most astute commercial decisions of his career – to build his own test tank. The Denny Tank was opened in 1883. It was 100 yards long and 7 feet deep and the firm were able to test their ships' future performance from scale models. One of the best illustrations of the advantage they gained from this was their contract from the Belgian Government for the *Princess Henriette* in 1888. Dennys accepted ruthless penalty clauses involving not only delivery date, but also minimum speed levels. The tank guaranteed success and the company delivered on time. The experiment tank survived through external orders until 1984, when it was taken over by the Scottish Maritime Museum. Visitors are able to see the model-making workshop with its original tools and equipment, the test tank and the upstairs drawing office where the complete records of every design tested are stored. The front of the building has a dedication to William Froude who inspired Denny to build this tank.

One of the strangest industrial enterprises in Dumbarton was

Dumbarton Rock and Governor's House.

the Kosmoid Company. Founded by a Dr Shiels, a pharmacist who ran nursing homes in Glasgow and London, the factory had some unusual features. The walls were exceptionally thick, constructed in reinforced concrete with steel girders while the doors were all lined with steel plates. It was believed to have been intended for experiments in the transmutation of base into precious metals – alchemy. In 1905, Dr Shiels had paid £12,000 to a John Melville for a formula to turn lead into mercury, then mercury into gold. Shiels managed to persuade several local businessmen to invest over £200,000 in this business before he was exposed as a fraud in 1906. The factory is now occupied by the more conventional Babcock and Wilcox Tube Works.

Dumbarton has also had some rather more distinguished citizens. Patrick Colquhoun (1745-1820) was born in Dumbarton, son of a tobacco lord. He went out to Virginia when he was 16, returning to Scotland in 1766 when he started a crystal glassworks at Verreville on the Broomielaw. He became Lord Provost of Glasgow on 1782, living in Kelvingrove House beside the river Kelvin. He was responsible for founding the Glasgow Chamber of Commerce, the first in Britain, and also for raising troops to fight the Americans in the War of Independence, which he realised would have a disastrous effect on trade. Colquhoun moved to London where he became a police magistrate and established the Thames River Police in 1796.

Robert Bontine Cunninghame Graham (1852-1936) was also prominent in public life but in a more political sphere. His grandfather had been an MP in the 18th century and had supported the French Revolution. Robert showed no early signs of being a political revolutionary, being educated at Harrow, then living as a rancher in Argentina until he was 31. He became a Liberal MP after he returned to Scotland, where, in 1887, he helped found the Scottish Home Rule Association. When the Scottish Labour Party was formed in 1888, he became its first president. He then gave up politics and started travelling and writing, being known particularly for his essays and short stories. When the Scottish National Party was formed in 1928, he became its first president, but he died in Buenos Aries in 1936. There is a memorial to him on Cardross Road.

The swift-flowing river Leven runs from Balloch on Loch Lomond a mere nine miles to the Clyde at Dumbarton. Its clean, fast-flowing waters made it ideal for use in the bleaching industry. The local landowners, the Smollett family of Bonhill, got a Government grant to lay out bleachfields in the Dutch style with channels of water running between hedges on which the wet linen was laid to dry. Mrs Smollett founded a village for the workers between the two fields of Cordale and Dalquhurn, naming it Renton after her daughter-in-law, Cecelia Renton. The industry expanded to include cotton printfields and in the 19th century, dyeing. Another new town was built to accommodate the ever-increasing workforce and was named Alexandria after Alexander Smollett. The industry expanded down to the Clyde where cotton bleaching and printing were carried on at Milton and Bowling.

One of the most famous buildings in the Vale of Leven is the erstwhile Argyll Motor Works, founded by Alexander Govan who had started producing cars in a small Bridgeton factory. In 1904, one of his cars did the journey from Land's End to John O'Groats in forty-two hours, an amazing achievement considering the state of the roads at the time. Another Argyll car broke the world record at Brooklands Racetrack in 1913. For a time the company had the highest production in Europe and employed the best craftsmen, not only mechanics and coachbuilders but also, in the

Clyde Navigation Trust Boundary Cross, Cardross.

finishing trades, coach trimmers and french polishers, all the latter being women. The firm became involved in a length and expensive litigation battle with Daimler over the use of a new sleeve-valve, which Argyll eventually won but the company never recovered from the cost of it. Tragically, it went into liquidation just a few weeks before the Great War began, an event which would have certainly saved it. The firm moved back to Bridgeton where it produced a few cars until finally closing in 1928. Govan himself had died suddenly of a stroke in 1907; Govan Drive and Argyll Street were named in his memory. The factory was taken over by an ammunitions firm in 1916, then by the Admiralty in 1935 as a torpedo factory, which closed in 1969. The space has now been divided up into more economically viable units and is occupied by several smaller firms.

Cardross

Until the parish boundaries were redrawn in the 17th century, Cardross Parish began on the western bank of the Leven. The ruins of a small church in Levengrove Park are the 14th century Cardross Parish Church. It was a small rectangular building with a square tower at the east end, where there is a monumental slab to the Dixon family, whose mansion formerly stood in Levengrove. Between Dumbarton and Cardross, on the north side of the A814, are the traces of the old raised beach, at the end of which lies the settlement of Craigend, where the second and third parish churches were built in 1644 and 1826. A village grew up around the site, although even by 1755 the population of the whole parish was still only 795. Several mansions were built in Cardross by owners of factories in Dumbarton and the Vale of Leven but the village itself never became industrialised. Workers from Renton and Alexandria would walk over Carmen Hill to church for communion, a custom which is thought to have started the traditional Cardross Whelk Fair. Workers would bring their families down to the shore to gather whelks and picnic on the beach. Later in the 19th century, booths were set up with food and amusements. The tradition eventually disappeared after the Great War. The large wooden cross on the shore marks the limit of the jurisdiction of the Clyde Navigation Trust.

The main occupation in the area was agriculture and much of the local farm produce was sent across the river to Port Glasgow and Greenock, river being easier than road transport. There were once five ferries operating between Craigend and Ardmore, each with an inn. The return cargo was manure from the streets of the towns which fetched the healthy price of two shillings a cart.

The opening of the railway in 1858 brought the biggest change to Cardross. It became feasible to live in Cardross and commute to Glasgow. This led to considerable middle-class housing being built in the area between the road and the railway line. Communication along the north became more important than across the river so the ferries and their inns disappeared. The new village was built mostly on the lands of Kilmahew which had been owned from the 13th century until 1820 by the Napier family. The remains of their castle on the north side of the golf course beside the Kilmahew Burn can still be explored although it is in a very ruinous and overgrown condition. The estate was bought in 1859 by James Burns who with his brother George joined with Samuel Cunard to found the Cunard Shipping Line. Burns built a new mansion at Kilmahew, designed by J.J. Burnet in Jacobean style. It was taken over by the Roman Catholic Church as a training college in 1948 and an architecturally acclaimed modern annexe was added to the eastern side in 1966. The training college has now closed.

Nearby is the much restored Kirkton or Kilmahew Chapel, dedicated to a follower of Saint Patrick – Saint Mochta or Mayhew. The first documentary evidence dates from 1370, but the discovery of a small incised cross slab suggests that it was a religious site from a much earlier date. The building was consecrated by the Bishop of Argyll in 1467, but after having been used as a school in the 18th and 19th centuries, it was left a ruin. Restored and reconsecrated in the 1950s its plain mediaeval style gives it a quiet, religious atmosphere.

Like many other Clydeside communities, Cardross suffered badly in bombing raids in the Second World War. More than sixty houses were damaged and the Parish Church was all but destroyed by incendiary bombs. After rejecting the feasibility of rebuilding, the congregation amalgamated with the Burns Free Church in Station Road, and made safe the ruins of the old church to stand as a war memorial.

Cardross is famous in sporting circles for its golf club which has produced many successful amateur players, for example, Charlie Green, a Scottish and British Amateur Internationalist and Suzanne McMahon, a successful ladies competitor. Golf started in Cardross in 1895 when a small six-hole course was laid out where Church and Reay Avenues are now. A new course was designed by Willie Fernie, a celebrated golfer, and opened in 1904. The club house was another victim of the Blitz and the club had to make do with temporary accommodation until 1956, when the new club house was built.

Nowadays, Cardross is a residential commuter village. Apart from the sawmill on the shore there is no industry. The modern housing estates are spreading further and further uphill to the back of the village and the old mansion houses have all been converted to institutional use.

Ardmore

Once an island, the attractive promontory of Ardmore juts out into the Clyde just to the west of Cardross. There is an easy nature trail of three kilometres around the perimeter with many interesting geological, botanical and ornithological features to look at. Several different habitats lie in close proximity, each with their own species: mudflats, acid moorland, meadow, shingle beach, farmland. Wear wellington boots as the going can get very muddy and be prepared to take to the edge of the fields where the shore path has been washed away. On the south shore is an unusual geological formation of Upper Old Red Sandstone rocks lying directly on top of Lower Old Red Sandstone, while on the north side are old sea cliffs, now well inland, which date from the time when Ardmore was an island. Botanically, the species range from the shore line flowers of thrift, sea campion and sea aster to acid soil plants such as heather and bog asphodel. Visit the area in early spring and see it glow with golden gorse bushes where greenfinches, stonechats, wrens and robins can all be seen. Round on the mudflats at low tide it is possible to see the remains of an old fish yair, a line of stones in a curved shape behind which fish, especially salmon, were trapped by the ebbing tide. The best way to observe the wading birds is to settle down when the water is at its lowest and watch as the incoming tide herds them towards you. There are often large numbers of oystercatcher, lapwing, redshank and, of course, gull.

Helensburgh

Helensburgh is situated right at the western tip of the north bank of the Clyde, a position which must have encouraged Sir James Colquhoun of Luss to build a new town here. He bought the lands of Malig from the Mcaulay family with the idea of establishing a planned village supported by a textile industry. A

Kilmahew or Kirkton Chapel, Cardross.

notice placed in the *Glasgow Journal* in 1776 advertised plots of land for sale, with particular encouragement to stocking, linen and woollen weavers, but no textile industry was ever established. However, the beautiful position of the town with its spectacular views in all directions attracted visitors and led to it becoming a popular holiday resort.

The town was named after Sir James' wife Helen and was created a burgh of barony in 1802. The wide streets were laid out in a grid pattern and hundreds of blossom trees were planted along them. One street was lined with laburnum trees which were later removed in case anyone poisoned themselves by eating the seed pods. By 1834 the population had reached 1,200 and 126 of the houses offered accommodation to rent. Like Cardross, the opening of the railway brought many more residents and the villas spread further up the hill, especially when a second railway line opened at the back of the town.

Between 1851 and 1861 the population increased by 65 per cent. The villas of upper Helensburgh form one of the most interesting and diverse collections of domestic architecture in Scotland. The most famous is the National Trust-owned Hill House, built for the publisher William Blackie in 1902 by Charles

Rennie Mackintosh. The house is still just as it was designed and is a wonderful opportunity to appreciate Mackintosh's ideas, unspoilt by later alterations. Every detail contributes to the total effect – the stencils, the fabrics, the furniture, even the light fittings. Unfortunately, the house is only open in the summer; in the winter it must suffice to admire the exterior from outside the garden wall. The White House in Upper Colquhoun Street dates from the same period and shows similar influences in design. Several other villas were designed by local architect William Leiper in a marked contrast of style – the outside walls are not harled but covered with decorative surfaces of brick, tile or half-timbering. Walk past Brantwoode and Strathmoyne in West Munro Drive, or Tordarroch in Douglas Drive. The Great War ended this style of living; the social climate changed and working in service was no longer a popular occupation.

Helensburgh's popularity as a holiday resort increased with the boom years of the pleasure steamers; trips 'doon the watter' became a favourite excursion. It is appropriate that one of Helensburgh's most famous residents was the steamship pioneer, Henry Bell. Born in Torphichen in 1767, he trained first as a millwright, then as a shipbuilder at Borrowstouness. After working for a short time in London, he returned to Glasgow in 1790. Knowing of William Symington and Patrick Miller's pioneering work with steam engines, he worked on his own design for a steam-powered paddle steamer – the *Comet*. The hull was built by John Wood of Greenock, the engine by John Robertson and the boiler by David Napier, both of Glasgow. The engine produced only four horsepower and a large squaresail was fitted to the tall smokestack to help in rough weather. After successful trials, by 1812 she was sailing between Glasgow, Greenock and Helensburgh. Bell decided to increase her length, an alteration which he carried out on the shore at Helensburgh. On a voyage to the West Highlands shortly afterwards, the *Comet* hit some rocks and broke where the new hull section had been inserted. Henry Bell was on board at the time and managed to salvage the engine which was later fitted into *Comet II*. The flywheel from this engine stands in Hermitage Park as a memorial to Bell, who died in 1830. He and his wife ran the Baths Hotel in Helensburgh, which stood where Queen's Court is now and he was the first provost of the town in 1807-10.

Hill House, Helensburgh, designed by Charles Rennie Mackintosh.

Helensburgh also saw one of the early steamer accidents when a small ship called the *Telegraph* blew up. It was a 118-foot coastal steamer, built in 1841, and it had plied successfully between Glasgow and Helensburgh for three years. It was tied up at the pier when its high-pressure boiler was allowed to go dry, causing it to explode and killing its owner, Mr Hedderwick, and several others.

Helensburgh is still popular as a destination for weekend outings and the front has many cafés and restaurants. This town marks the end of the Lowland communities; beyond here the road turns north towards the Highlands while the river opens out to the south and the Kyles of Bute.

CHAPTER 12

Erskine to the Cloch

Beneath the Erskine Bridge on the south shore of the river lies the Princess Louise Scottish Hospital, or Erskine Hospital as it is better known. During the Great War, because the existing military hospitals were swamped with casualties, Glasgow surgeons, led by Sir William McEwan, campaigned for a new hospital in the west of Scotland. With great generosity, Erskine Mansion was offered to them rent-free by its owner, Thomas Aikman, with an option to buy at a very reduced price. The house and 360 acres of grounds were purchased by a gift of Sir John Reid, while public donations poured in. A sum of £200,000 was raised in a few weeks. The hospital received many gifts in kind – pianos, typewriters, a snooker table, even a cow! When the first patients started arriving the surgeons found that they had a problem obtaining a supply of artificial limbs which, until 1916, had come from abroad. Sir William appealed to the engineers of Clydeside for their technical help. Limbs made to the highest specifications were manufactured and supplied at cost price by firms such as Yarrows, Stephens, John Browns, and Dennys. By October 1918, 2,697 men had been given new limbs.

Between the two wars, the Hospital's main function changed from surgical to long-term care of the permanently disabled. Erskine suffered a shortage of funds and had to launch new appeals. Sir Harry Lauder gave a concert for them – his son John had been killed in 1916. Many years later, John's fianceé, Mildred Thomson, bequeathed £80,000 to the Hospital in his memory. The launch of the Queen Mary gave them another opportunity to raise money as their grounds were an ideal place to watch the ship being towed down river. They charged a small entrance fee on which the Inland Revenue tried to tax them, but an appeal against this charge was successful. Over the years many new buildings and facilities have been added: workshops where the men can continue with old skills or learn new ones, a gymnasium to help with physiotherapy, cottages in the grounds where ex-servicemen and their families can live. It is no longer just a

Garden statuary, Finlaystone House.

hospital, but also a community and home to almost 400 men.

Finlaystone

The Finlaystone Estate lies just to the west of the village of Langbank. It was once the seat of the Cunninghams, Earls of Glencairn and is now the home of the chief of the Clan Macmillan, General Sir Gordon Macmillan. The grounds are open all year round and visitors are made very welcome. Various walks and trails have been marked out through the lovely woodland and landscaped gardens and there is a ranger available to give talks, information or guided walks. The present Finlaystone House was remodelled by J.J. Burnett at the turn of the century, and incorporates an earlier Georgian house within the new building. One of the window panes in the library is etched with the signature of Robert Burns who was entertained here by the 14th Earl. Robert Burns named his son John Glencairn in his honour. The estate produces large crops of strawberries and raspberries, a legacy of the market gardens which used to be so common in the area. Port Glasgow was renowned for its magnum bonum plums and for its strawberries, which after the railway opened in 1841, were sent as far away as Covent Garden Market in London. The farms were only cleared away by the expansion of the shipyards in the 1860s.

Reminders of another once-thriving local industry lie along the shore. At low tide lines of wooden posts are exposed. They are the remains of four miles of timber ponds where imported timber from North America was stored to season or until required by the shipyards. Before the 19th century, timber had come from the Baltic and Norway but with the tremendous growth of ship-building in wood, the timber trade with North America became more important, and, in 1825, 19,650 tons of timber were imported. It came in logs, the full length of the trees, which were unloaded through portholes in the bows of the ships directly into the river. Each log was measured and numbered before metal rings were driven into each end. The logs were then chained together into rafts and towed to the timber ponds. The measurers owned this timber and rented the ponds from the ground superiors. There was some risk involved as it was not unknown for a bad storm to cause the logs to break free, and sometimes even block the river. The average surface area of each pond was between seven and eight acres, for which the annual rent was approximately £100. The business declined drastically with the change to iron ships although one company, Carsewell and Son, managed to survive until 1941.

To the east of the timber ponds are mudflats which have been designated a 'site of special scientific interest' because of the large number of wildfowl and waders which feed there, particularly in the winter. The most common are shelduck and eider in the

Dovecot, Newark Castle, Port Glasgow.

water, while the most frequently-seen waders are redshank, dunlin and plovers. The shore is not easy to reach here and involves a 'dice with death' dash across the A8. It is safer to go down to the shore at the junction of the Bishopton road and walk west from there.

Port Glasgow

Entering the town now, it is hard to believe that this was once a prosperous pretty place. It had elegant public buildings such as the 18th century Newark Parish Church and the Town Buildings: alas, both are now in a sad state of dilapidation. This impression of past glory is increased by the view of the architecturally impressive Gourock Ropeworks factory, seven storeys of tall red brick, but obviously derelict. The town is divided into two parts:

the older section on the raised beach, a narrow strip of land between the river and the cliffs, and the newer section, where modern housing schemes sprawl back on to the moors. Between the two, tenements cling precariously to the cliff face.

The best preserved of its historical buildings is Newark Castle, one of the finest examples of 16th century domestic architecture in the west of Scotland. It consists of three sides of a square, a 16th century L-shaped building connecting two earlier square towers. To the east of the main building, at the edge of the shore, is a beehive dovecote. This castle was the home of the Maxwell family, until George Maxwell Napier was forced to sell it in the 18th century. He is reputed to have been particularly extravagant where horses were concerned; he shod one with silver shoes when he rode to collect his bride from Caithness. In the 19th century the castle was divided up and rented to several occupants. One of these was a rope-spinner called John Orr who had a sideline dealing in wild animals which he bought from incoming ships. In 1830 he advertised a young leopard and bear for sale in the *Glasgow Herald*. The Castle has survived so well because it has always been kept wind and water tight. It has also been protected from the land-hungry shipbuilders who wanted it demolished. Newark Castle is open to visitors during the summer months.

The fortunes of Port Glasgow have always depended on the river. Even their food staples had to be imported by boat, mostly from Ireland, because the farms on the hilltops could not produce enough to feed the local population. Riots broke out in the early 18th century when the government made the importation of certain foodstuffs illegal, but the smugglers did well out of it.

Fishing was never a major industry in Port Glasgow, even when the herring were plentiful, most of the herring curing being done in Greenock. Because so much salt had to be imported for this, James Crawford of Gartnavel tried to manufacture it locally but could not produce enough to make it an economically viable business. Salmon were plentiful but were caught in yairs on the shore rather than from boats. To procure fat for the soap factories, Greenock and Port Glasgow combined to send out a small whaling fleet. The blubber was sent out to Glasgow for processing, but this business too proved unprofitable and was abandoned.

Old Kirk, Nelson Street, Greenock.

The village of Newark owed its good fortune in becoming the main trading port on the Clyde to being the highest navigable point for cargo boats on the river before Dumbuck sandbanks. Having deep water close to shore made it the ideal site for the

Glasgow merchants to establish their New Port Glasgow and most based their headquarters there too. Improvements were made to the harbour, and storage facilities were built both for bonded goods and for goods awaiting re-export to the European markets. In 1793, of all the locally-owned ships, 16 were employed in herring fishing while 91 were involved in foreign trade. The harbour was further extended in 1838 to provide a spacious new dock, but disaster struck only one year later. A steamer called the *British Queen* had a new engine fitted by crane at the dockside and just after she sailed, the quay collapsed. Not enough funds could be raised to repair it so the dock gates were left open and the bay became a tidal harbour once more.

The earliest shipbuilder in Port Glasgow was the famous John Wood, who laid the hull of the *Comet*. A replica of this first sea-going steamship was built at Lithgow's yard on the 150th anniversary of its launch and is on display, rather incongruously, in the middle of the town centre car park. John Wood specialised in building sailing ships and river steamers. In 1817 he built a small steamer called the *Tug* for coastal trade on the Forth. It proved unsuitable for that purpose and was used for towing instead, thus giving the name 'tug' to all towing vessels.

His brother, Charles, became involved in the timber trade and went over to Canada. In 1824 he built a special ship of undressed uncaulked timber which was launched loaded with a full cargo of pine deals, making her almost unsinkable. The intention had been to break her up when she arrived in England, the ship itself being part of the cargo, but somebody foolishly decided to try sailing her back to Canada again with chalk as ballast. This of course soaked up water which poured through the uncaulked timbers and the ship foundered in mid-Atlantic.

In 1839, another yard, John Reid and Company, started business, One of their most famous contracts was to build a floating church for the Free Church congregation at Strontian, where the proprietor refused to rent them any land. One of Reid's apprentices, William Lithgow, set up the shipbuilding yard which was to overshadow all others in Port Glasgow. With Russell and Rodger as partners, he started in the Bay yard in 1874 but bought them out in 1891. Lithgow's two sons expanded the business, absorbing other companies such as steel stockholders James Dunlop and Fairfields Shipbuilders. The shipyards are all

The Tontine Hotel, Ardgowan Square, Greenock, originally home of Greenock merchant, George Robertson, built 1808.

closed now apart from small repair businesses and the new industries are in the estate on top of the cliffs at Devol, a riverside site being no longer an advantage.

Greenock

Port Glasgow and Greenock are now contiguous, but in 1700 Greenock was only a single row of thatched houses along the shore with no harbour and overshadowed by its more prosperous neighbour. Now it is a town of spires and churches with some of the most elegant 19th century streets in Scotland. The new town plan designed by David Reid in 1818 has largely determined the shape of Greenock today. A simple grid layout with wide streets and generous house plots has given the town a unique and elegant appearance. In Shaw Place is a line of five Georgian town houses with columned entrances built in 1830-5. The tenements down Brisbane Street lead the eye to the Old Kirk, a copy of London's St Martin's in the Field, built in 1840 with a tall central steeple added in 1850. In complete contrast, on the opposing corner is Ardgowan Hospice, a red-brick Free Style cottage with a bright and decorative emblazon above the window. Around

Ardgowan Square are an interesting selection of buildings: the impressive Tontine Hotel, Georgian town houses, the later Victorian Renaissance style Greenock Club.

The first harbour, West Harbour, was opened in 1710, financed by a local tax on brewing malt. One year later the oldest and longest surviving family shipbuilding firm, John Scotts, was opened. During the 18th century there were eight small shipbuilding firms spread along the shore from the Bay of Quick to Cartsdyke, building small wooden ships for the coastal trade or the herring fishing. In the history of Inverclyde, over ninety shipyards have operated at one time or another, but at least half of these lasted less then ten years. Scotts was always a pioneering yard; they built the first graving dock, now threatened with destruction by dockside developments, in 1767; the *John Campbell* was the first ship to be launched fully rigged and masted in 1806. Early in the 19th century they bought Brownlie's Foundry and began their own marine engineering firm. During the First and Second World Wars the yard built submarines, cruisers and destroyers for the Royal Navy, then in the postwar period found a new market in passenger-cargo liners for the Far East trade. Appropriately, as Greenock's other well-known industry is sugar refining, Scotts designed and constructed the first custom-built sugar carrier, the *Crystal Cube*. The shipbuilding yards are all closed now, and the last of the large marine engineering firms, Clark Kincaid, have just announced their closure. A massive Clydeside industry which employed thousands of men, produced millions of tonnes of shipping and made more than a few fortunes is disappearing rapidly. The survivors have no security; they hold their breath waiting for the next contract, and closures and redundancies are always in the news. To survive, towns whose economies were based on shipbuilding and engineering are looking for new employers and industries. Greenock is now the main container terminal on the Clyde, but this is no longer a labour intensive business. To the south-west of the town in Spango Valley lies the enormous IBM complex: computers are the new growth area of the 20th century.

Another product for which Greenock is famous is sugar. The first sugar house was built in 1765 when all the raw sugar cane came from the West Indies and the industry expanded rapidly in the 19th century as the taste for sugar increased. By 1850 the

Greenock refineries were the largest outside London. The working conditions were so bad that few local people would take the jobs in the refineries. They had to rely on immigrant Irish labour. In 1855 sugar beet was introduced to Britain from Europe, and the market was flooded with cheap sugar, which put many of the Greenock refineries out of business. The survivors were saved by the Brussels Convention in 1902 which imposed import controls. Now only Tate and Lyle's refinery is left,

In the early 19th century, seventy people were employed by the Straw Hat manufactory, making plaited straw hats copied from the Leghorn design. Scottish rye grass was sent up to Orkney to be plaited, a skill used there for chair-making, then sent back to Greenock to be made into hats. The owners of this business, James and Andrew Muir, having capital profits to invest, decided to diversify into pottery manufacture. This was an expanding market as people changed from wooden tableware to pottery. The Muirs took on James Stevenson, a Staffordshire potter, as a partner to operate the factory. The Clyde Pottery Company survived until 1905 through several changes of ownership and financial difficulties. It produced some very attractive tableware and examples of it are on display in the Maclean Museum in Greenock, including a Toby jug in its different phases of manufacture.

Ironically, in a town with a high annual rainfall of 60 inches, Greenock has had problems maintaining an adequate water supply. In the 17th century drinking water was taken from wells sunk in various parts of the town. Because of the rapidly increasing population by the end of the 18th century ways of increasing the water supply were urgently sought. James Watt built two small reservoirs above the town which brought some more water down to the wells, but the relief was temporary. From 1813 there was extreme overcrowding in the town and living conditions were appallingly insanitary. The report in the *First Statistical Account* complains of blood and filth from the slaughterhouse being discharged through the town. Not surprisingly there were frequent outbreaks of infectious diseases such as cholera and smallpox. Drastic action was obviously needed. Robert Thom was a civil engineer and proprietor of a cotton works in Rothesay, for which he had ensured a good water supply by means of a system of aqueducts and sluices.

Timber ponds and the Clyde Pottery, Greenock, 1883.

Thom was asked by Greenock's MP, Sir Michael Shaw Stewart, to survey the ground above the town with a view to building a similar system for Greenock. Thom surveyed the area in 1824 and produced a plan to supply Greenock with enough water to satisfy both industrial and domestic demand even in the driest of weather. A large reservoir was created by damming the source of the Shaws river in the hills behind Inverkip. This water was then carried by an open aqueduct to a small reservoir at Overton, from where it was taken down to the town in two branches, with falls of varying heights to supply different power levels to suit different industries. Drinking water was taken through a 15-inch square stone aqueduct buried underground and through three slow filters, giving Greenock its first clean water supply. The sluice gates were officially opened on the 16th April 1827 by Greenock's Chief Magistrate, William Leitch, who then proceeded to float down the first stretch of the Cut in a small boat gaily decorated with flags. Among the industries built on the eastern falls were sugar refineries, flour mills, woollen mills, and paper works, an iron foundry and a chemical works. The largest water wheel used in the system was 70 feet in diameter and 12 feet broad, and was built for the wool-spinning factory. There is no doubt that Thom's water scheme contributed enormously to the industrial expansion of the town. The Cut supplied the town until 1968, when it was decided to bore a tunnel from Loch Thom through the hill to the Long Dam at Overton, a project which was completed in July 1969. The Greenock Cut has been designated an 'ancient monument' and it is possible to walk the length of it from the Visitor Centre at Cornalees Bridge at the north-western corner of Clyde-Muirshiel Regional Park. The Park stretches across the West Renfrew Moors from Greenock to Lochwinnoch, and although most of the land is privately owned, visitors are actively encouraged. The Visitor Centre at Cornalees has an enthusiastic ranger service and informative displays about the Cut and the wildlife around it. Scheduled as a 'site of special scientific interest', there are many interesting plants and birds to look out for.

Gourock

Gourock lies on two circular bays contiguous with Greenock and has two separate shore lines to either side of the railway pier. Gourock Bay faces to the north with dramatic views across the river Clyde to Rosneath and Ben Lomond. West Bay faces west towards Strone, Dunoon and the entrances to Holy Loch and Loch Long. Gourock escaped the horrors of intensive indus-trialisation suffered by her neighbours. While the Gourock Ropeworks started here in 1777, making ropes and sails for the maritime trade, the company expanded to larger premises in Port Glasgow. The original ropewalk in Gourock was 400 yards long and the firm employed 50 people.

Gourock was already a holiday resort by 1792. The minister reported that a number of houses were kept solely for renting by families from Glasgow attracted by the sea-bathing. In the *New Statistical Account*, written almost forty years later, summer visitors are mentioned again: 'The poor in this place have great advantages from the strangers who resort to it for sea-bathing quarters, who are very kind to them'.

Gourock Pier was constructed by the Caledonian Railway Company who had bought the harbour in 1869 but did not start building the wooden steamboat wharf till 1886. To bring the railway through from Greenock, a tunnel a mile and a half long, the longest in Scotland, had to be constructed, Before the railway were allowed to operate the steamers, they had to set up their own limited liability company, The Caledonian Steam

Gourock Station and Pier.

Packet Company, and operated such famous steamers as the *Ivanhoe* and the *Duchess of Rothesay*. Now it is the car ferry terminal for the crossing to Dunoon, and summer cruises to the Kyles leave from it.

Just south of Gourock, beyond McInroy's Point, is the Cloch Lighthouse, designed by Robert Stevenson and Thomas Smith. The tower is 80 feet high, with lightkeepers' cottages and store-houses clustered around its foot, although the light is now automatic. The Cloch has a fixed white light, visible for 14 miles, which is paired with the Gantocks Light at Dunoon to warn approaching shipping that they are entering the River Clyde. This narrow passage has seen many shipwrecks. Many still lie in the water to be explored by divers and avoided by seamen. Three ships lie off the Cloch Point: the *Catherine;* the *Europa;* the *Portland*. The *Catherine* was a wooden sloop en route from Iona bringing Highland farm workers down to Greenock for the harvesting season of 1882. It was run down by a steam tug, the *Hercules,* and sank immediately in deep water. Forty-two people were drowned. The *Europa* was an iron cargo ship sailing from

Glasgow to Malaga in 1884 when it collided head on with the S. S. *Roseville* bound for Glasgow with a cargo of barley. The latter managed to beach and was subsequently repaired, but the *Europa* sank with a loss of five lives. The *Portland* sank in 1907 when it collided with a schooner in heavy fog.

Further Reading

G. Blake, *The Gourock*. Gourock Ropework C.A. Port Glasgow, 1963.

J. Butt (ed). *Robert Owen: Prince of Cotton Spinners*. David and Charles, Newton Abbot, 1971.

A. Fisher, *William Wallace*. John Donald, Edinburgh, 1986.

A.F. Fraser, *The Native Horses of Scotland*. John Donald, Edinburgh, 1987.

J. Hood, *History of Clydebank*. Parthenon, Carnforth, 1988.

L. Keppie, *Scotland's Roman Remains*. John Donald, Edinburgh, 1986.

R.K. Marshall, *The Days of Duchess Anne*. Collins, London, 1973.

I. Macivor, *Craignethan Castle*. HMSO, Edinburgh, 1978.

R. McLellan, *Linmill Stories*. Canongate, Edinburgh, 1990.

I. Macleod, *Discovering Galloway*. John Donald, Edinburgh 1990.

I. Macleod, *Glasgow in Old Picture Postcards*. European Library, Zaltbommel, The Netherlands, 1984.

I. MacPhail, *Short History of Dunbartonshire*. Spa Books, Stevenage, 1984.

G. Parsonage, *Rescue His Business, The Clyde His Life*. Glasgow City Libraries, Glasgow, 1990.

S. Pollard and J. Salt (eds). *Robert Owen. Prophet of the Poor*. Macmillan, London, 1971.

A.M. Scott, *Clydesdale*. Thornton Butterworth, London, 1924.

W.D. Simpson, *Bothwell Castle*. HMSO, Edinburgh, 1988.

A. Smart, *Villages of Glasgow*. Vol. I. John Donald, Edinburgh, 1988.

J.B. Stevenson, *Exploring Scotland's Heritage. The Clyde Estuary and Central Region*. HMSO, Edinburgh, 1985.

F.A. Walker, *The South Clyde Estuary – An Illustrated Architectural Guide*. S.A.P., Edinburgh, 1986.

F.M. Walker, *Song of the Clyde*. Patrick Stephens, Cambridge, 1984.

Ancient Monuments of Clydesdale. Clydesdale D.C., Lanark, 1989.

Historic Buildings of Clydesdale. Clydesdale D.C., Lanark, 1987.

Lanarkshire. An Inventory of the Prehistoric and Roman Monuments. RCAHMS, Edinburgh, 1978.

Index